To John Ba...

With all good wishes

Molly Sedgwick.

2nd November 1996

WHEN THE 'CHUTE WENT UP

WENT UP

· Adventures of a pioneer Lady Parchutist ·

WHEN THE 'CHUTE WENT UP

WENT UP

• Adventures of a pioneer Lady Parchutist •

DOLLY SHEPHERD
with **Peter Hearn** & **Molly Sedgwick**

SKYLINE

First published in Great Britain in 1984 by Robert Hale Ltd
This revised edition published in 1996 by Skyline Publishing
Chapel End, Littleworth, Amberley, Stroud GL5 5AL

© Dolly Shepherd, Molly Sedgwick & Peter Hearn

All Rights Reserved. Except for brief quotations for review purposes, this
book or any part thereof, must not be reproduced in any form without
permission in writing from the publisher.

Designed by John Christopher, Designworks
Printed in Great Britain by Bookcraft

ISBN – 1 874180 01 6
(Autobiography & Aeronautics)

*Dedicated to all parachutists
past, present and future*

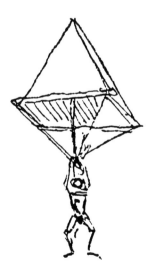

Leonardo da Vinci's sketch of a parachute circa 1485

Contents

Preface

In the history of the parachute there was a time when, before it could come down, the 'chute had to go up – suspended beneath a gas or hot-air balloon, ready to be released when the aeronaut was at the required altitude. There was no pack for the canopy and lines. There was no harness for the parachutist: just a 'sling' to help take the weight of the body and a trapeze bar to hold on to.

This was the age of the balloon, before the aeroplane captured the skies. It was an age of great elegance and serenity, perhaps symbolized by the balloon itself, so majestic and unhurried. It was an age when the parachutist, smartly attired, would spend an hour or more strolling amongst the crowds as they gathered to watch the inflation and preparation of the balloon, making friends and establishing a personal relationship with the spectators before the event, then returning to the arena to celebrate with them afterwards. It was altogether a more leisurely time.

I suppose, within two months of my ninety-seventh birthday, I must be one of the very few survivors of that band of Edwardian parachutists who entertained the crowds at fêtes and pleasure grounds throughout the country during the first decade of the century. When it was first suggested that I should recount some of my experiences, I felt that they were too insignificant to be of interest to others, particularly in view of the achievements of today, when thousands of girls think nothing of flinging themselves from planes in free fall. However, I have finally been persuaded that there may be some who would be amused to hear of those distant days 'when the 'chute went up...', so I have pieced together some of my early adventures. These are not necessarily in chronological order, as in places I have grouped together incidents and anecdotes with similar themes in an attempt to convey both the hazards and the pleasures of being a pioneer Edwardian lady parachutist.

Fortunately, I still have a good memory and a number of photos and press cuttings to help me, and I am amazed at the amount of interest, assistance and co-operation that we have had from people all over the country – a few of whom still remember me! However, if my reminiscences are not accurate in the finest detail I hope I shall be forgiven for, after all, it did happen eighty years ago!

The book would not have been written at all if it had not been for the persistence and encouragement of my daughter Molly, who also carried out much meticulous research and wrote the original story. I am also grateful to Group Captain Peter Hearn, a pioneer free-fall parachutist and author, for helping me to put the story into its final form. To Alan Scott, yet another parachutist, go my thanks for his illustrations in the book.

I am grateful to all those who have given me active encouragement, and should like to thank in particular the following people who have assisted me with practical help in one way or another: Mrs G Baker, Mr J Bryant and Mrs J Cheesman (Chatterley Whitfield Mining Museum), Mr G Bruce (late of Short Bros), Mr K Kissack and Miss E Williams (Monmouth Museum), Mr C Williams (Tamworth Library), Mr C Carrington for permission to quote from his book *Alexandra Park and Palace, A History*, Mr V Tyrrell of the Reference Library Stoke-on-Trent, Mr C McCann, and members of the Red Devils parachute display team.

Molly Shepherd

(Elizabeth Sedgwick)
Eastbourne, September 1983

①

Table Number Five

I was born on 19 November 1886 in Potters Bar. Whilst I was still very young the family moved to Southgate. It was still a rural area then. I was christened Elizabeth Mariam, but when my grandmother saw me for the first time, she declared that I looked like a 'little dolly'. 'Dolly' I have been ever since. I was always something of a tomboy – a rather daring and impetuous young girl. These characteristics landed me in quite a few scrapes. For instance...

My brother David, who was four years older than me, suffered from some form of weakness so that if he received a blow on any part of the head, his nose would bleed severely. I would then have the unenviable job of holding his head back with a series of ice-packs on his forehead, for half an hour or more, until the blood ceased gushing from his nose. My mother and I were used to ministering to him, but it was a horrifying sight.

So, when his schoolmaster gave David a box-on-the-ears – no doubt well deserved – and he returned home pumping blood, I was so incensed that the next day I marched angrily into the boys' school. I had no idea what I was going to say, but when I entered the classroom and saw the master standing there in a pale suit, I had a mental flashback to the previous day's 'bloody' scene at home. I caught sight of an inkwell and quite on impulse picked it up and threw it at him. My aim was true, for it splashed all over that immaculate suit! I was, of course, expelled.

The only other place that would have me after that was a Catholic school, three and a half miles away. It was considered a fitting punishment that I had to walk there and back for the rest of my schooldays – but what happy days they were!

My brother had some influence on my adventurous spirit and physical aptitude. He was forever daring me to match him in various escapades, such as climbing trees, sliding down drainpipes and doing acrobatics on a clothes-line. He even challenged me to jump from a low roof with a carriage umbrella for support. Quite inadequate support it was, too!

It was from my parents, however, that I undoubtedly inherited those characteristics that were to lead me into and see me safely through so many adventures. My father, a Somerset man, had a fine physique and commanded great respect as a member of the Metropolitan Police, in which capacity he did a lot of plain-clothes detective work. He was a first-class sportsman, known for his cricketing prowess as 'WG' after the great W G Grace. He was a man of immense courage. There was an occasion when a house in the village caught fire, and we hurried to the scene to join the crowd that was waiting for the two-man fire brigade to arrive with their pushcart and pumps. We all thought that the house was empty until a cry rang out, "Little Georgie is still in there!" Without hesitating, my father dived into the flames and smoke. When he emerged, he had 'Little Georgie' under his arm – but he no longer had his fine beard and bushy eyebrows! He was a kind and gentle person, with a wonderful sense of humour. It was from him that I developed the habit of talking and singing to myself in times of trouble.

Courage was also one of my mother's attributes. I remember the night when she saw the silhouetted figure of a man lurking in the vegetable garden. Thinking that it was an intruder, she rushed into the darkness and set about him with a poker – to find that it was a scarecrow that my father had erected that afternoon. My goodness, she never lived that down! She was also a fearless horsewoman and was never so happy as when she was up at Jennings' Farm, helping to break in the wild ponies that Farmer Jennings had bought from the New Forest. Like most others, we of course had our own pony and trap, there being no motor cars at the time.

Yes, I was blessed with fine parents, both inherently kind and with a Christian outlook. My mother was very good to the neighbours, always being ready and willing to help anyone when called upon, day or night.

However, our upbringing was strict – almost spartan, particularly for me as the middle of three children. My sister, Wene, the baby, was seven and a half years younger than me. She was christened Miriam Elsie, but once again it was Grandma who named her for life. "What a weenie little thing," was her remark on first seeing her. 'Wene' she was called for the rest of her life. She was always such a good little girl and *never* needed to be reprimanded.

Although my mother was a kind person, she never stood any nonsense! In the morning she would call my brother and me at about six-thirty. She would call us once. If we were not up within ten minutes, she would come up again – with a big sponge of icy cold water. I had only one dousing! But many times my brother would call out, "Doll – Mum's coming up!" Like lightning we were out of bed.

I also recall a lunchtime when I decided that I didn't really fancy the boiled beef and carrots that my mother had prepared for us. There was no fuss. She just took it away. But there was no pudding for me. And at tea time, there was my boiled beef and carrots – cold. I still didn't eat it. Nor at supper, when it appeared again. When it was put before me at breakfast the next morning, however, I wolfed it down. Never again did I say that I didn't like anything!

We were also given responsibility at an early age. When I was eight, it was my job to go down to the common with a bridle to catch the pony and ride him home, bare-back. When I was nine, my mother bought a Singer sewing machine. She happened to be out when the lady called to show her how to use it, so I took the lesson instead and as a result was given the job of making the family underwear.

On reflection I am sure that the disciplines and early responsibilities of our childhood prepared us well for later life. Certainly, by the age of sixteen I was tall, mature and very self-assured for my age, and I had a definite mind of my own.

So it was with firm intentions and great confidence that, on a pleasant spring day in 1903, I boarded a train from New Southgate for the $1^1/2$d.* journey to Wood Green, there to join a very festive throng making their way up the hill to the Alexandra Palace.

The 'Ally Pally', as it was affectionately called, was one of London's most popular entertainment centres of the time. People of all classes, ages and interests would flock there – over a hundred thousand of them on Bank Holidays, at weekends and for special occasions. It had everything! Within the extensive grounds there was a racecourse; a large fairground with swings, carousels, steam gondolas, switchbacks and all the traditional fun of the fair; a boating lake; a conservatory; and various enclosures given over to carnivals, processions, military tournaments, demonstrations of a joyous or political nature, balloon ascents and magnificent firework displays – frequently produced by James Pain or C T Brock, whose families have carried on the tradition to this day. The Great Hall with its grandiose organ was the venue for major musical presentations, and the smaller Bijou Theatre produced a wide variety of shows by touring companies. The Alexandra Palace had also become a thriving centre for aerial activities, with its large Banqueting Hall used as a workshop by a small group of dedicated aeronauts who, in their enthusiasm to defy gravity, were thought by most people at that time to be quite eccentric.

The 'Ally Pally' had experienced a chequered history. It was said that during its construction in 1862, on 150 acres of land provided by descendants of Cecil Rhodes, a supposed witch had been evicted from her home on top of the hill. Under-

Throughout the book I use the old £ s. d. notation, whereby one shilling represents 5p.

standably upset, she laid a curse on the project. It seemed to have had some effect, for sixteen days after its opening on 24 May 1873, the original Palace was completely destroyed by fire. Nor were its troubles over. Rebuilt and opened to the pubic in 1875, it suffered a series of financial crises in spite of its popularity and was forced to close in 1889. Under new management it was opened to the public again nine years later. When the Alexandra Palace was again gutted by fire in 1980, one might have wondered if the old witch was still at work!

On that fine day in 1903 when I made my way up the hill there was certainly nothing to suggest that the dear old 'Ally Pally' was under a witch's curse. There was a general air of contentment and anticipation amongst the happy throngs, brought about as much by the fine weather and the bright flowers in their fresh colours as by the prospects of the entertainments that lay ahead.

However, it was not solely for entertainment that I was there that morning...

My prime purpose was indeed to attend the concert that was to be given that afternoon by the great American 'March King' – John Philip Sousa. He was one of the musical sensations of the day, having taken the country by storm with his 'Washington Post', 'Stars and Stripes Forever' and 'The Star-Spangled Banner'. Wherever he went he was received with tremendous enthusiasm, so it was little wonder that the tickets for the series of concerts that he was to give in the Great Hall were sold out. No recordings or radio in those days – if you wanted to hear the great musicians of the time, you had to go to their concerts. Even had tickets been available, I could not have afforded one, but I was quite determined that I was going to see and hear the great Sousa, ticket or no ticket.

Pushing my way through the jostling crowds, I made straight for an unpretentious side entrance to the basement of the Great Hall. It was the door used by the staff, and by those seeking employment by Bertram, the official caterers. It was a Mr Fox, I understood, who was all powerful in the appointment of waitresses to work in the refreshment area of the Great Hall, and it was in search of him that I directed my youthful but nonetheless determined tread. Mr Fox was a middle-aged man, genial and short of stature. He must have liked the way I smiled, for when I boldly informed him that I was seeking a position as a waitress in the Great Hall, he granted my request forthwith, engaged me at a salary of 1s. 3d. per day and told me to report immediately to the manageress in the refreshment area. This I hastened to do before he might change his mind.

The manageress obviously thought that I was an experienced waitress, and I did not seek to disillusion her. I was already wearing a black alpaca dress that reached to my ankles, and to go with this she gave me a white fancy apron, which tied at the back with a large bow. To wear beneath it I was given a little cream bag in which to put my tips – usually of a penny, I was to discover. The manageress then gave me the briefest outline of my duties and indicated the four tables to which I had been assigned – numbers five, six, seven and eight. Without more ado she turned her attention to other matters. Thus I became a waitress in the Great Hall!

My boldness had paid handsomely, and I reflected on my good fortune as I laid up my four tables – by watching carefully what the other girls did. The refreshment area was at one side of the auditorium, with a long marble-topped counter catering for tea and coffee at one end and cold drinks – alcoholic and otherwise – at the other, with cakes and sandwiches displayed on a stand between them. There were altogether twenty tables where waitress service was offered. From the refreshment area a good view could be had of the stage, which had been graced by the leading names in the world of music, such as Sir Henry Wood, Clara Butt, Charles Copland, John McCormack, Mark Hamburg and Kreisler. For an Easter performance of Mendelssohn's *Elijah* it had housed an orchestra of 120, with 1,800 singers. Now the great Sousa was to take the platform, and I was to have a view of the occasion that was both first-class and free!

I was not disappointed. No refreshments were served during the performance, so that I was able to stand by the counter to watch the entire show. I was absolutely captivated by the music, and by the conductor himself. He held his audience spellbound by his capacity to change mood and atmosphere with a wave of his magic wand. Though rooted to the spot, his movements had all the grace of a ballet dancer. Under his superb direction the orchestra played a wide selection of pieces, both popular and classical, but it was the unforgettable Sousa marches that so electrified the large audience.

All too soon the concert ended. The last strains of 'Stars and Stripes' seemed to linger in the hall as though held there by an audience reluctant to let them go, but I was brought from my trance by the sudden realization that I must now earn the privilege of being there, for there was a purposeful movement towards the refreshment area. The members of the orchestra had already vacated their places, and as I prepared myself for the fray, I wondered where the 'March King' himself had disappeared to. But he hadn't disappeared at all. I suddenly saw him making his way through the crowd towards the refreshment area, modestly acknowledging the applause of those around him. How graceful and dignified he looked in his closely tailored uniform and with his greying beard. Then to my delight and considerable surprise he took a seat – at table number five! The great Philip Sousa was sitting at one of my tables! I could scarcely believe my good fortune, and my heart missed a beat as I heard the soft American voice requesting my attention.

As I hastened to serve him, he was joined by three other gentlemen. The first I already knew – the hard-working Director of Entertainments, Mr John Henderson. Then, with hurried steps, followed a dapper little man with clear, piercing eyes and a neat moustache with waxed ends. When he spoke, it was with a good command of the English language but with a delightfully soft accent that indicated his French origins. He had a parachute emblem embroidered on the top lapel of his smart blue jacket, an anchor on the lower lapel, and a balloon on his navy blue peaked cap. I realized that this must be the celebrated Auguste Gaudron, the parachutist and balloonist who had so often thrilled the crowds at the 'Ally Pally' and elsewhere with his daring aerial performances.

There was no mistaking the next man to join the group at table number five. With long hair flowing to his broad shoulders, he sported a large waxed moustache and neatly trimmed goatee beard, and was attired in a large cowboy hat, buckskin breeches and jacket, and high boots with silver spurs. It was the famous Samuel Franklin Cody, namesake of the original 'Buffalo Bill', William Frederick Cody, whom he met from time to time, and like him, a flamboyant showman who had transferred the riding, roping and shooting skills that he had used as a Texas cowboy to the European showgrounds and theatres. His stage production – *The Klondike Nugget* – was at that time playing at the Bijou Theatre. S F Cody was more than a showman, however, for he was also one of that small band of aeronautical pioneers who were using the Palace as a base in their attempts to gain mastery of the air.

What a tableful of celebrities I thus found myself catering for on my first day as a waitress! My service must have been satisfactory, for this distinguished quartet subsequently made table number five all their own, and I became a delighted attendant at their animated and wide-ranging discussions.

I had to work hard for those pleasures. The hours were long – ten in the morning until nine at night, with a two-hour break. The two concerts by Sousa were the highlight of the day, and I was well contented despite my aching feet. I was disappointed of course when the concerts by the 'March King' came to an end and the Great Hall no longer resounded to the stirring marches, the romantic waltzes and the scintillating rhythm of whatever music the maestro chose for our entertainment.

After the departure of Sousa, the other three men continued to meet regularly at table number five. There was usually an effervescent atmosphere brought about by the animated exchange of ideas, with the discussions accompanied by vivid gesticulations, especially on the part of Cody, whose enthusiasm for the potential of the man-lifting kites that he was constructing knew no bounds. Such was the zeal of the aeronauts that it was quite infectious, and I found myself drawn increasingly into their conversations and deliberations, so that I became a fourth – albeit an 'upstanding' – member of their party.

One day the cheerful mood that usually prevailed at table number five was gone. Gloom and despondency reigned. Cody's handsome face was wreathed in frowns as the others listened with concern to his story. One of the acts featured in *The Klondike Nugget* was a sharp-shooting display by Cody himself, in which he shot an egg from the top of his wife's head. It appeared that during the previous evening's performance the bullet had grazed her scalp. "She cannot appear tonight – which means that part of the show can't go on. It has never happened before…" he concluded, with a sad shake of his head. His obvious and uncharacteristic dejection touched my heart, and without hesitation I interrupted their conversation.

"I'll do it for you," I said. "I'll come tonight."

Three pairs of incredulous eyes were raised to mine. "Would you really?" said Cody. "Do you mean that?"

His expression turned to one of grateful relief when I assured him that I did indeed mean it. He and Mr Henderson – as Director of Entertainments – were delighted, and no time was lost in making arrangements for me to be free from my duties in the Great Hall that evening. I wondered what I had let myself in for, but I was not unduly nervous. The stage held no fears for me, as I was not without experience before an audience. Only a few months previously I had answered an advertisement in the paper seeking 'girls for pantomime'. I had been auditioned, accepted and given the part of Captain Jolly Roger in *Robinson Crusoe*, in the very Bijou Theatre where I was now to appear with Cody. For a girl of my age and background it had seemed a rather daring thing to do, but I had thought that it might be good fun. And so it was! I had only one speaking line, which was, "Hi Hi Captain, and what shall we do with the women?" In stage whispers just loud enough for me to hear, the 'pirates' grouped around me on the set left me in no doubt what they would like to do with the women! After that I was given minor parts in several dramatic productions such as *The Shaugran* and *Under The Red Robe.* In one of them I became a corpse, an illusion which I rather spoilt on one occasion with an explosive sneeze! Like a true professional, the leading actor grasped the chenille cloth from a nearby table and threw it over me. What the producer said to me afterwards does not bear repeating! Otherwise, my acting was good enough for Mr Henderson to ask me if I would like to go on tour. My aunt happened to be visiting us that day and was so shocked that she pointed out in no uncertain terms some of the pitfalls that awaited a young actress on tour, so I did not pursue my theatrical ambitions any further.

No, I was not at all worried about appearing on stage, and even the nature of the act did not frighten me, for Cody's reputation as a sharp-shooter was second to none. One of his acts was to hit a ball off his own head by shooting at the trigger of a rifle held in a vice at the other side of the stage, previously set to aim at the ball. Shooting an egg off *my* head, I therefore assumed, would be quite straightforward. Nevertheless, I took along my friend Emily Turner for moral support. Emily was one of the waitresses with whom I worked. The manageress, also thinking that I might need a companion, had given her time off from work to accompany me, but as it turned out it would be Emily who needed looking after!

We arrived at the Bijou Theatre at the appointed time, to be met by Vivien, one of the two Cody boys who appeared in the show with their parents. He escorted us to the front of the house and gave me an enormous box of chocolates.

"What a dear little theatre," whispered Emily. The Bijou certainly was a cosy place. It always had a friendly atmosphere, which now added to my confidence. I had not seen *The Klondike Nugget*, so had no idea what to expect. The minutes ticked by until suddenly the elegant Master of Ceremonies was saying, "You are about to witness one of the greatest feats to be performed by that crack-shot, the famous Buffalo Bill, who will shoot an egg off a lady's head. Will the lady please come forward."

I handed the precious chocolates to Emily and mounted the stairs on to the stage, with head held high as I tried to look as unconcerned as I could under the circumstances. Cody, dressed in his flamboyant cowboy style, led me to my spot and carefully placed the egg – made of a resin-plaster compound – on my head. "Keep quite still," he said softly. Then he took up his own position about fifteen feet in front of me. Slowly he raised his trusty Winchester rifle to his shoulder and took aim. "This is it," I thought. But it wasn't. From the wings came young Vivien Cody and proceeded carefully to blindfold his father. Coo, I hadn't expected *that*! I must admit that the butterflies became quite busy in my tummy at that moment, but the rifle was unwavering, and I did my best to emulate it. Vivien stepped back. Hardly daring to breathe, I kept my eyes firmly fixed on the marksman. There was a sudden CRACK, and the egg burst into fragments, which scattered to the floor around me. From the auditorium came cries of relief and loud applause. There was considerable relief on the stage too, I can tell you! When I returned to my seat, I found Emily on the floor and the chocolates scattered all around her! The poor girl had fainted clean away and was being revived with smelling-salts.

Well, I was quite a heroine, and in his gratitude Cody rewarded me by asking if I would like to view the kites that he was developing, and to be shown around the aeronauts' workshop in the Banqueting Hall. It was an offer that I jumped at, and one that was to open the door to adventures beyond my wildest dreams.

At the earliest opportunity Cody escorted me into this strange world where man's eternal quest to rise into the air was being realized by this handful of devoted aeronauts. It must be remembered that this was the spring of 1903. No aeroplane had yet flown. No one had yet heard of the Wright Brothers, who later in that year, on 17th December, would achieve immortal fame with the first powered flight in a heavier-than-air machine – of 852 feet. Where man was concerned, the sky still belonged to the balloon, to the parachute, to the very earliest dirigibles, and to the man-lifting kites as developed by Cody.

He had become fascinated by kites when, as a fourteen-year-old 'wrangler' in charge of the horses on the great Texan trail drives, a Chinese cook had shown him how to fly simple devices made of sticks and oiled paper. After an eventful career as cowboy, trail-boss, buffalo-hunter and bronco-buster, he had brought his Wild West skills to Europe, where his sharp-shooting acts and his well-publicized pony races against champion cyclists had attracted huge audiences. He had not lost his interest in kites, and during the Boer War he had tried to persuade the Army of the potential of man-lifting kites for observation purposes. The authorities had shown little interest, so Cody had financed his own aerial experiments from the proceeds of his shows. By 1901 he had developed a system which used 'lifter kites' to hoist a cable into the air, up which a huge nineteen-foot box-kite could carry a passenger in a wicker basket-seat to heights of a thousand feet or more. Cody possessed no technical qualification, but he had a most inventive mind and was in no doubt that with further development he would be able to add power to his kites and set them free from the cable – actually to *fly*! This, of course, he was eventually to achieve when in 1908 he built and piloted the first heavier-than-air machine to fly in Britain. In 1903, however, such aspirations were thought by most to be those of a crank.

I was full of excitement when Cody showed me into the aeronautical workshop. The hall, some two hundred feet long and sixty feet wide, was a hive of industry. In addition to Cody's great kites there were the limp forms of parachutes hanging from the ceiling; balloons collapsed in lifeless heaps or stretched out on the floor; various huge wicker baskets; piles of netting; hanks of rope and cord of all dimensions. There was an indefinable smell, composed of glue and canvas and hemp and dust, and the incessant chatter of sewing machines presented a constant background to the bustle of human activity.

With undisguised enthusiasm, Cody explained to me the technicalities of his beloved kites. He even allowed me to sit in one of the wicker seats suspended beneath an enormous box-kite that had the presence of some prehistoric flying creature. He assured me that the only other lady to have done so – and indeed to have made several ascents in the apparatus – was his wife. Lela Cody was a very brave women, who played an active role in her husband's twin interests – the stage and the air. The story was told of an occasion when Cody asked her to make an ascent under one of his kites for a test that he was conducting. When she was hoisted some five hundred feet into the air, he went into the workshop to make some minor adjustment to a piece of gear and became so engrossed in what he was doing that he completely forgot the good lady until her cries for attention eventually reached him!

It is unlikely that he would have let me sit in the machine had I been wearing any green, for he had a superstitious aversion to the colour. Poor Cody! Ten years later he was to die in the splintered wreckage of one of his own aircraft. With him died his passenger, W H B Evans, the Hampshire cricket captain – who was found to have green in his socks. On the day that Cody talked to me with such enthusiasm and optimism in the Banqueting Hall of the 'Ally Pally', however, his greatest aerial triumphs and ultimate tragedy lay in the unknown future.

Cody introduced me to Harry Spencer, one of three brothers whose father and grandfather before them had been engaged in the making and piloting of balloons for almost a century. Mr Spencer explained to me his high hopes for the dirigible that he and Monsieur Gaudron were constructing for Dr Barton in a specially built shed close to the hall.

Then it was Monsieur Gaudron himself – or 'Captain' Gaudron as I was to come to know him – who continued my conducted tour of the workshop. As a balloonist and parachutist of note, he was well known at the Alexandra Palace. At the reopening of the site to the public at Easter in 1898, the balloon ascents and parachute descents that he made with his compatriots Mademoiselle Alma Beaumont and Captain Charles Lorraine had thrilled the crowds of a hundred thousand. His performances had remained a popular attraction ever since.

I was fascinated by his explanations of the techniques and

sensations of parachuting from the balloons and, being of an inquiring mind, I plied him with questions. He sensed my growing interest in this particular activity and, with a twinkle in those keen eyes, he eventually asked a question of me.

"Would *you* like to make a parachute descent?"

I didn't hesitate. I didn't need to think about it. My response was spontaneous and emphatic.

"Yes," I said.

Little did I realize what adventures one little word could lead to...

John Philip Sousa

Monsieur Auguste Gaudron

Samuel Franklin Cody

2

The Aerial Showmen

In 1903, when Captain Gaudron issued that startling invitation, parachuting from balloons was in its heyday as an aerial spectacle. Indeed, it was the only aerial spectacle of the time, for the aeroplane had not yet taken to the sky, and the various forms of glider that immediately preceded it were not adaptable to public performance. The aerial stage belonged to the balloonist and the parachutist.

No major outdoor entertainment or fête was complete without its death-defying aeronaut. They really were thought to be defying death, too, for the realms of the air were still little explored and imperfectly understood. The sky was a place of mystery and hazard, and the intrepid few who ventured into it were accorded the adulation that astronauts first attracted.

The parachute and the balloon had grown up together, and by the time I made their acquaintance they were not much more than a hundred years old. The balloon was the senior partner in this relationship and had played a far more important role in aeronautical development. It had been the first to take the stage when, on 5 June 1783, the Montgolfier brothers – paper-makers of Annonay in France – sent up the first hot-air balloon, and on 12th September launched the first aerial voyagers: a sheep, a cock and a duck. When the travellers were recovered from their basket after landing, the cock was found to be the worse for wear. It was decided, however, that this was not the consequence of its aerial adventure, but that it had been trodden on by the sheep, so the way seemed clear for the first human to take to the air. So hazardous did this still appear that Louis XVI at first insisted that the passengers should be condemned criminals. However, one of Montgolfier's assistants – Jean François Pilâtre de Rozier – persuaded the monarch that the honour of being the first man *"de s'élever dans les airs"* should not go to a common villain, and volunteered himself for the flight. Thus it was on 21 November 1783 he and his equally brave companion the Marquis d'Arlandes became the first men to break free from the earth and rise into the oceans of air. This they did beneath a balloon made of linen and paper, fuelled by the hot-air from a suspended brazier. The aeronauts were armed with bundles of straw to feed the fire, and a pail of water and a sponge apiece to dampen its ardour should it become excessive.

De Rozier was not only the first man to taste the freedom of the air: he also became its first victim when in 1785 his attempt to combine the lifting properties of hot-air and hydrogen in one balloon ended in inevitable disaster in the skies above Boulogne.

By that time, however, commissioned by the Académie Française in Paris, Professor Jacques Charles had, on 27th August of the same year, developed and successfully flown a hydrogen-filled globe, built by Jean and Nicolas Robert, and on 1st December, together with the older of the Robert brothers, he had ascended from the Tuilleries to make the first manned flight with a hydrogen-filled balloon. These 'Charlières', with obvious advantages for more sustained and less hazardous flight, soon replaced the 'Montgolfières' as the primary vehicle for lifting an increasing number of adventurous spirits into the unknown reaches of the sky. Amongst them was Madame Thible, who in 1784 in Lyons became the first woman to ascend in a balloon. In that same year the handsome young Italian Vicenzo Lunardi made the first balloon ascent in Britain, followed shortly afterwards by James Sadler, the first British aeronaut. The first English lady to be borne aloft as a passenger was Mrs Sage, who subsequently reported "...I was infinitely better pleased than I ever was at any former event of my life".

And what of the parachute at this time?

In purely theoretical terms, the concept of a 'fall-breaker' preceded the balloon. It is perhaps not surprising to find that in the early sixteenth century the fertile mind of Leonardo da Vinci had sketched and described a 'tent roof of calked linen' beneath which a man might '...let himself fall from any great height without danger'. There is nothing to suggest that Leonardo, or any of the other theorists who followed, put their 'fall-breakers' to the test. This was probably just as well.

It was not until the late eighteenth century that the parachute as we know it today began to take shape. The Frenchman Louis Sebastian Lenormand designed a 'dome' of impermeable linen attached by numerous lines to a wickerwork seat. In 1783 he tested his device by launching several un-impressed animals from the tower of the Montpellier observatory, and it was he who gave the parachute its name (para – against/avoid, and chute – a fall). Montgolfier adopted the idea, and after carrying out similar experiments by dropping a sheep from the tower of the Papal Palace in Avignon, he actually advocated the parachute as a means of escape from a balloon, but he did not say or demonstrate how this might be done.

The first to bring the parachute and the balloon together was yet another Frenchman, Jean Pierre Blanchard. One of the most prominent aerial showmen of those pioneering years, he had been the first to cross the English Channel by balloon in 1785 – only just, for he had to throw everything from the basket, including his jacket and breeches, to keep the balloon in the air as it approached the French coast. As an added attraction to his balloon ascents, he made a parachute, braced like an open umbrella, that could be suspended beneath the balloon basket and released at will. A succession of dogs and cats proved the efficiency of this apparatus, but Blanchard was not inclined to emulate them.

It was not until 1797 that man first entrusted himself to a parachute. It is said that André Jacques Garnerin, whilst imprisoned in a fortress in Buda during the French Revolution, had contemplated the possibility of escaping from his confinement with some form of 'fall-breaker'. No doubt many others before him had entertained such fancies, but he was the first to put them into subsequent practice. Already with some experience as a balloonist, and with some knowledge of Blanchard's exhibitions, he made a parachute with a round canopy suspended like a shower curtain from a large disc at the apex, with a central pole rather like an umbrella handle, and thirty-six lines attaching the periphery of the canopy to a small one-man basket. The whole assembly was designed to be hung beneath a balloon, then cast adrift to fill with air after it had been hoisted to a sufficient altitude. This is exactly what Garnerin did in Paris on 22 October 1797, to oscillate rather wildly back to earth as the world's first parachutist.

It was a momentous achievement, but one that no other aeronaut was in a hurry to copy. Garnerin himself repeated the feat only occasionally – six times in all, over a period of seven years. One who followed this brave pioneer was Jeanne Labrosse, the first woman parachutist, subsequently to marry Garnerin. She made only the one descent, but his niece Elisa was to become a more active jumper, the first professional parachutist, with thirty-nine performances throughout Europe during the period 1816 to 1836.

It was Garnerin who made the first parachute descent to be seen in Britain, when he ascended from the Volunteer Grounds near Grosvenor Square in London on 21 September 1802, and came back to earth in his little basket with such a violent pendulum-like motion that he was subsequently sick over those who sought to carry him from the scene in triumph.

Garnerin eventually solved the problem of oscillation by introducing a vent in the crown of the parachute canopy. An alternative solution was proposed by that great aeronautical theorist Sir George Cayley who – after watching Garnerin's descent – suggested that stability could be achieved if the parachute were constructed in the form of an *inverted* cone. Another who had witnessed Garnerin's drop and had come to the same conclusion as Sir George was a gentle artist called Robert Cocking. Unfortunately for Cocking, he was one of the

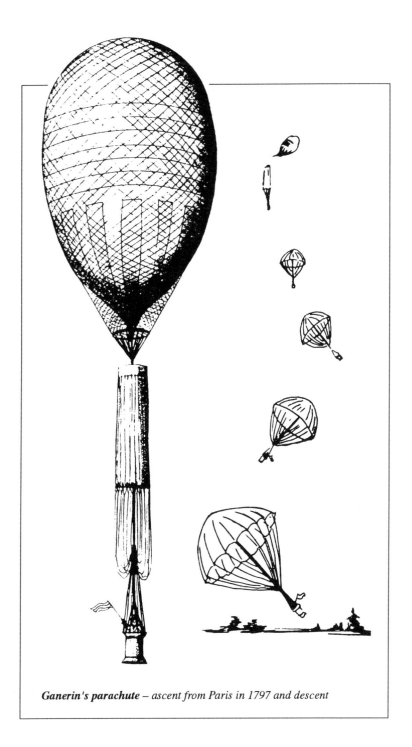

Ganerin's parachute *– ascent from Paris in 1797 and descent*

very few who at the time were prepared to put theory into practice. He did not do so until thirty-five years later when, at the age of sixty-one, in 1837, he ascended from Vauxhall Gardens with a parachute made of twenty-two panels of Irish linen stiffened into the shape of a shallow funnel with wooden struts and large hoops of tin and copper. The whole assembly weighed over two hundred pounds and was hoisted aloft beneath Charles Green's giant *Nassau* balloon – named after its epic eighteen-hour flight from London to Weilburg in the European province of Nassau in 1836. With Charles Green in the balloon basket was Edward Spencer, grandfather of the Harry Spencer whom I met that same day that Gaudron asked me if I would like to make a parachute descent.

Both Green and Spencer had reservations about Cocking's escapade, and even during the long ascent they tried to dissuade him from the venture. The aspiring parachutist, however, lacked neither determination nor courage, and just over a mile above Lee Green in Kent he bade goodnight to the two balloonists and operated the liberating cord. For a moment the parachute dropped steadily. Then the wooden ribs and the three large hoops slowly buckled inwards under the pressure of the airflow on the fabric covering. Still in his tiny basket and perhaps wondering sadly where his calculations had gone wrong, Robert Cocking hurtled to his death beneath the tattered, wildly flapping remnants of his invention.

Such was the publicity given to this tragic event that it lingered in the public memory for a long time and gave to parachuting a reputation that was not altogether deserved. Other would-be parachutists were therefore actively discouraged from taking to the air for many years. However, when the aeronaut John Hampton, shortly after Cocking's death, sought to use his newly designed parachute for the first time, the gas company in Cheltenham refused to fill his balloon for the ascent. They eventually agreed to do so on the understanding that he would make only a tethered ascent. Tethered it was – until he cut the rope. Having risen to a sufficient height, he then released himself from the rogue balloon and descended to earth, and to

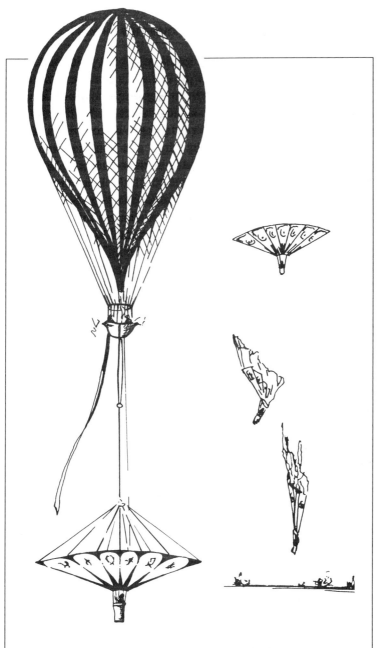

Cocking's parachute *– ascent under the Nassau balloon in 1837 and fatal descent over Lee Green*

the applause of the crowd, under a parachute of whalebone-stiffened canvas, to become the first successful British parachutist in October 1838. He went on to gain a reputation as the 'Tea Garden Entertainer', by ascending for most of his exhibitions from the tea gardens that were so popular in London at the time – places such as Cremorne, Vauxhall and Montpellier Gardens. My Uncle Will often used to go to Cremorne Gardens during its later years as an entertainment centre, and saw several aerial performances there. He was never particularly impressed. 'Mountebank stunts' he used to call them.

Although considered one of the foremost parachutists of his time, Hampton made only seven descents during his aeronautical career. The fact is that parachuting remained an infrequent form of entertainment – and that is all it was, pure entertainment. It served no scientific or military purpose and, unlike the balloon, contributed little to the development of aeronautics during those years. Apart from the use of small 'chutes dropped from balloon baskets to aid in the assessment of wind strength and direction at lower altitudes, the parachute was purely a vehicle for showmen, and as such it was still a cumbersome device of uncertain habits, and not always popular with authority. Even its value as a life-saver as advocated by Montgolfier had not been pursued, for as the gas balloon was developed it was found that in the event of an accident it became its own 'fall-breaker' when the deflated bag became trapped in the upper part of the netting to provide a quite effective canopy.

In France, the Godard and Poitevin families continued the Garnerin tradition, but elsewhere, discouraged by authority and without scientific inspiration, there was little activity and no advance in the parachuting field. It was a time when there were plenty of theorists, but few practitioners.

Then, in the 1880s, there appeared on the scene a new concept that was to revolutionize aerial showmanship. It was born in America, fathered by a showman of Dutch extraction and considerable girth called Park van Tassel. He produced a 'chute of heavy canvas and manilla rope, designed to be suspended from a fixed point by a 'break cord', to hang in a completely limp state, with none of the hoops and discs used by Garnerin to hold it partially open, and none of the 'stiffening' of the canopy adopted by Hampton and most others. The theory was that, when released to be dragged earthwards by the weight of its human load, it would be forced open by the air rushing up into the mouth of the canopy. There would be no need, thought van Tassel, for any of the cumbersome and artificial opening aids that had so complicated the traditional semi-rigid parachutes. He also replaced the basket with a bar for the parachutist to hold on to, and a simple sling for him to sit in – a device with which I was to become very familiar!

The first to demonstrate the van Tassel 'chute in public was a wire-walking acrobat called Thomas Scott Baldwin. On 30 January 1887 he jumped successfully from a tethered balloon before some thirty thousand people in San Francisco's Golden Gate Park. When he parted company with van Tassel after a difference of opinion over his share of the profits, he took with him the Dutchman's idea of the flexible parachute, improved upon it and patented his own design in 1888.

In that same year Baldwin brought his new parachute to Britain for a series of exhibition jumps at the Alexandra Palace, which at that time was losing money and in need of some added attraction. Baldwin certainly provided that! The announcement of his intentions stirred great interest, not all of it favourable. There were still those who remembered Cocking. In the House of Lords the Earl of Milltown asked the Government: *"...whether the attention of the Home Office had been directed to an announcement in the papers that Professor Baldwin would, at the Alexandra Palace on Saturday next, jump out of a balloon at a thousand feet above the ground; whether it was believed that the announcement was genuine, and if so whether measures would be taken to prevent so dangerous and demoralising an exhibition"*. He was assured that the police had been instructed to keep a close eye on the proceedings. What marvellous publicity all this provided! Londoners flocked in their thousands to see this crazy American risk his neck.

The Earl of Milltown need not have worried, for, amidst scenes of unrivalled enthusiasm, Baldwin made a total of twelve descents during the next two months, culminating in a Royal Performance before the Prince of Wales, later to become King Edward VII. The exhibitions were the subject of much controversy, loudly voiced in the newspapers. Whilst there were those who praised the parachutist's *'iron nerve, coolness, self-reliance and judgement'*, others *'regretted that the Alexandra speculation has to resort to the wretched sensationalism that is the curse of London entertainment'*. Tom Baldwin loved it all! Whilst some demanded his arrest, the Balloon Society awarded him their gold medal in recognition of his contribution to aeronautical science!

Whilst the controversies were raging, Baldwin was asked to attend the Middlesex Magistrates Court which was hearing the annual application of the Alexandra Palace for the renewal of its entertainment licence. On being asked if it was true that he descended by parachute holding on only by his hands, and with no safety device, he admitted that it was so, but added that *"...it was almost as impossible for him to let go as it was for any gentleman on the Bench to lose a grip of his senses"*. Renewal of the licence was granted. Baldwin went on to appear in several other British cities before setting off on a tour of Australia and the Far East as the first show-jumper of international repute.

In Britain and America the Baldwin exhibitions caused an immediate and remarkable revival of interest in parachuting as a spectacle. His flexible parachute was shamelessly copied by a growing number of imitators, as was his use of the hot-air balloon as a cheaper and sometimes more convenient alternative to the gas balloon as a means of carrying the parachutist into the air. Amongst those who followed Baldwin's lead in Britain were the Spencer brothers of Highbury, who added the manufacture and use of parachutes to the ballooning activities that had become a well-established family tradition. Like Baldwin, they toured the Far East. On one occasion in Malaya, when Harry Spencer at last tracked down a balloon that had drifted on its way after he had released himself for his parachute descent, he found that he was too late: the balloon had already been converted into shirts and sarongs!

A friendly rival of the Spencer brothers was a young Frenchman who had served his apprenticeship in balloon-building at the Lachambre balloon factory in Paris before becoming a resident in Britain at the age of twenty-two. He had first appeared as a balloonist and parachutist at the Alexandra Palace in 1898, and had been a regular performer there ever since. He had gathered to him a group of like-minded aerial adventurers, and his 'team' of parachutists was well known throughout the country at a time when parachuting from balloons was in its heyday. He was, of course, my new-found friend Monsieur Auguste Gaudron.

Gaudron was never to receive the recognition that was due to him as an aeronaut, perhaps because his greatest achievements in the field of lighter-than-air flight coincided with the birth of the aeroplane, which tended to steal the limelight. At the time that I joined the team, he was one of the most experienced parachutists in Britain, an outstanding balloonist, and one of the three leading makers of balloons and parachutes in the country – the others being the Spencers and the Short brothers. His association with the former was made even closer when he married their sister. In addition to his exploits as an aerial showman, Gaudron was at the forefront of airship development in Britain. As early as 1898 he had experimented with a powered balloon at the Alexandra Palace, and he was then involved with Harry Spencer in the construction and piloting of Dr Barton's dirigible. It was also with Dr Barton that he had 'delivered' the first airmail letters over Britain in his special 1902 *Coronation Balloon*, the *Mammoth*, throwing packets of one hundred specially printed and stamped postcards, attached to small parachutes, from the balloon basket at intervals over various towns and villages. The finder would take them to the nearest Post Office and they would be delivered the following day. At the time that I made his acquaintance, even greater achievements lay ahead of this dedicated aeronaut.

3

Into the Sky

When Captain Gaudron had asked me if I would like to make a parachute descent, I had been quite prepared to do so the very next day, but it was to be a long time before the opportunity arose.

Shortly after my visit to the aeronauts in the Banqueting Hall I left the 'Ally Pally'. My aunt, who owned the Ostrich Feather Emporium in Holborn, had been so horrified at the idea of my going on tour with the theatrical company that she had offered to teach me the ostrich feather trade and the manufacture of the feathers from their raw state to the exquisite creations of fashion in those Edwardian days. At first I travelled daily from Southgate, but soon arrangements were made for me to join my aunt in London.

Aunt Mariam – always known simply as 'Aunty' – was my mother's oldest sister. As the head of the family she was always consulted, and what she said really counted. She was a beautiful woman, with peaches-and-cream complexion, rosebud lips and a crown of golden hair. She had a tremendous sense of humour, and when she gave a hearty laugh, all her thirteen stone would shake! I had always loved visiting Aunty and Uncle in their beautiful home, where as a child I used to romp with their cat and dogs, and even ride on the back of one of their enormous St Bernards, Nero and Satan. Now I was most happy to be living with Aunty, although I was to find that her affection for me was to become somewhat possessive.

When work permitted, we would take a cab or landau up

to the Palace to enjoy the various entertainments. On occasions I would see Captain Gaudron there, but nothing was said about my aerial aspirations, and I assumed that he had forgotten all about our conversation. Thus it was to my surprise as well as to my delight that a year later I received a letter from him asking if I was still interested in making a parachute descent. I was not to know at the time that Gaudron was seeking a replacement for one of his team of aeronauts, a girl called Maud Brooks, who had been seriously injured in a parachuting accident.

My response was immediate and enthusiastic. Of course I was still interested! An appointment was made for me to see Gaudron, and it was with a beating heart and bubbling curiosity that I made my way once more to the aeronauts' workshop in the Banqueting Hall of the Alexandra Palace.

Although he displayed all the courtesies usually associated with the French, Captain Gaudron was a man of action rather than words. He certainly wasted very few in introducing me to the skills of parachuting! After greeting me, the first thing he did was to ask me to take hold of his hands and squeeze them as tightly as I could. No, it was not a gesture of Gallic familiarity. He was merely satisfying himself that I possessed the main asset of any parachutist of that era – a strong grip. He then took me to where a parachute was suspended, the folds of heavy silk and the cords hanging limply. Attached to the cords (nowadays they would be called rigging lines) and about six feet from the ground swung a wooden trapeze bar about twenty inches long. I was instructed to grasp it and take the full weight of my body on my arms. I did so, and hung there, feeling rather silly, while he watched intently for several seconds before nodding approvingly and allowing me to resume a more ladylike posture with my feet on the floor.

Apparently satisfied that I would not go plummeting straight to my death when suspended beneath a parachute, he came straight to the point. Would I, he asked, like to join his team of aeronauts? After I had gained some experience, I would be required to give shows in different parts of the country throughout the summer months. The prospect of becoming a *regular* parachutist was too good to be true! To travel as well – that was something that I had always wanted! Without hesitation I assured him that I would be most happy and honoured to join the famous Gaudron team.

"But what about training – and clothes?" I added.

"We will see to that now," he said, and without more ado my instruction began. Basic in the extreme, it lasted no more than half an hour.

"The important thing is to know how to fall," explained the master parachutist, and proceeded to give a practical demonstration. The secret was to roll on to the back as soon as the feet met the ground, and to throw the legs upwards immediately – even to go right over in a backward roll. This would spread the impact on to the shoulders instead of subjecting the legs to the whole shock.

"Never land 'standing up'," I was warned. "Now you do it."

I practised the fall several times. It was not difficult. All those tomboy activities into which my brother had led me were obviously going to come in useful, I thought. I was next taken back to the suspended parachute. This was how it would hang from the balloon, already stretched out for the ascent. There was no pack for it in those days. Nor was there a harness, just the trapeze bar and, trailing from it, cords and a strip of webbing about six inches wide, forming a type of sling. Captain Gaudron showed me how to step into this sling and demonstrated how it would rise up between the legs when the trapeze bar was raised above the head and would eventually take the weight of the body suspended beneath the parachute.

"You must take a very firm hold on the bar at all times, to maintain your balance," he advised.

He then drew my attention to a leather belt that could be worn round the waist and fastened to the bar with a snap-clasp. He explained that, because there were still those who thought that parachuting was excessively dangerous, the belt was sometimes worn to placate a particularly anxious public, and that I would certainly have to wear it for my first descent. "After that, you may please yourself," he added, in a tone that suggested that he considered such a device to be altogether superfluous.

I was next taken to one of the huge baskets that, suspended beneath the balloon, would be the carriage for my first journey into the skies. I was informed that it would take three or four passengers in addition to myself and the pilot, who would of course be the good Captain himself on this occasion.

"It will be what we call a 'right-away' balloon," he said.

"Why 'right-away'?" I asked.

"Because after you have jumped, it goes 'right away' with its passengers, to land further on."

He explained how the apex of the parachute would be tied to the netting of the balloon at its equator by a piece of cocoa string, which would snap as soon as the weight of my falling body was put on it, thus allowing the streamed parachute to break free and fill with air. To show how easily the string would break, he twisted a piece around his fingers and snapped it – just the way the grocers did in those days after they had weighed, packaged and tied up a packet of cocoa: hence 'cocoa string'. I was then shown how I would sit on the rim of the basket during the ascent, with legs dangling over the side, one hand clutching the trapeze bar and the other gripping the supporting ropes.

"When we are high enough, I will tell you to go, and you will just jump forward from the basket – like this!"

It all looked very easy – down there on the ground. I wondered if it would be so easy up *there*. The Captain must have read my thoughts.

"Will you be afraid?" he asked.

"No, of *course* I won't be afraid!" I replied, trying to convince myself as well as the Captain.

"The day before you jump – *then* you will worry," he said, with a twinkle in his eye.

He went on to tell me that after I had jumped I would probably land about a mile away from our point of departure, depending upon the strength and direction of the wind. I would be picked up by somebody with a pony and trap and returned to the enclosure to 'show myself' to the people. I sincerely hoped that I would be in a fit condition to 'show myself'. In full flow, he explained how later on I would need to learn more about the operation of the balloon itself, in preparation for making solo descents.

"And now to the uniform," he said.

The Captain was obviously very particular about the appearance of his team. My uniform would comprise a navy-blue knickerbocker suit with gold trimmings and a badge representing a parachute on the lapel of the jacket. There would be a high-peaked cap with a balloon insignia on it. I was directed to obtain these from Brittain's of Aldgate Street, where they made the gold insignia for naval uniforms, and I was advised to wear high-legged boots. It all sounded very swish.

And that was it. That was the sum total of my parachute training!

As I left the workshop for the sunlight outside, I turned my face towards the skies. Next time I came to the 'Ally Pally', I would be up *there*... up with those puffy little clouds wandering so serenely across their blue field... until the Captain's order came to jump! What *was* it going to be like? What *was* it going to be like?

In high spirits and hardly able to contain my excitement, I hurried to my aunt's home and banged in through the door.

"Guess what, Aunty!" I blurted out. "I'm going to make a parachute descent!"

Bubbling with enthusiasm, I proceeded to tell her of the arrangements that I had made to join Gaudron's team and to make my first jump at the 'Ally Pally' the following weekend. Then I noticed the expression on her face. My voice faltered and stopped.

In icy tones she said, "If you *do* go ahead with these mountebank stunts, you will never enter my house again." Then she turned and left the room.

It was like a dousing from my mother's ice-cold sponge at half-past-six in the morning. Mountebank stunts? I had never thought of parachuting as such. It just seemed like an exciting and challenging adventure to me. Rather daring and un-conventional, yes – but surely not *that* bad? I realized that my aunt was acting in what she truly believed to be in my best interests, just as she had done in dissuading me from touring with the theatre company; but this time I was not to be so easily deterred. I was torn agonizingly between my great affection for Aunty and my new-found ambition to join the aeronauts. My mind was soon made up. I had, after all, given my word to Monsieur Gaudron.

Aunty suffered from a badly ulcerated leg which I used to dress for her at least once each day. During the following week, and in secret, I was busy rolling bandages and preparing a stock of the necessary dressings and lotions. Two days before I was due to appear at the Palace, I led my aunt to the cupboard outside the bathroom.

"Aunty," I said, opening the cupboard door, "there are enough dressings and lotions here for at least three months."

"What the hell's that for?" came the astonished reply. My aunt never did mince her words.

"I'm going to make my first jump in two days' time, and as you said that I should not enter your house again if I did so, I've prepared a good supply of everything for dressing your leg."

Aunty, unusually for her, was stunned into silence. We stared at each other for the best part of a minute before she burst into tears and threw her arms around me. When she regained something of her composure and had wiped her eyes, she said, "Very well – you can go up, but *never* talk about it. Just tell me a few days before you are going, but *never* talk to me about it."

I was sorry that she disapproved so vehemently and that I would not be able to share my experiences with her, but I accepted her terms, and we were friends again.

The way was open to the skies above the Alexandra Palace.

The appointed day dawned fair. As I made my way up the hill from the station with the usual throng of pleasure-seekers, I

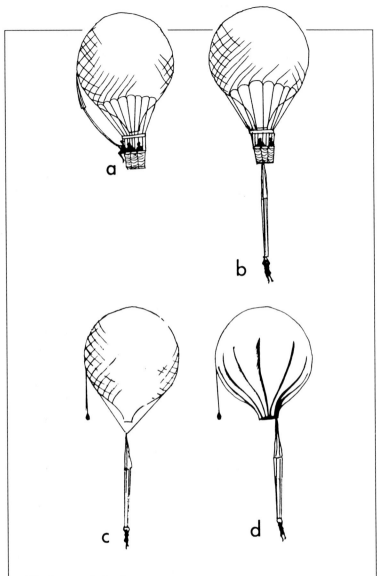

The four methods of ascent:
a. *On the side of the basket of a 'right-away' balloon*
b. *Suspended beneath the basket of a 'right-away' balloon*
c. *Suspended beneath a 'solo' gas balloon*
d. *Suspended beneath a 'solo' hot-air balloon*

realized that I was no longer one of them. I was to be one of the attractions, not one of the spectators. Soon I would be the centre of interest to many of these happy folk around me. I didn't really feel as though I deserved their attention, for I was just a young girl bent on adventure.

As I changed into my aeronautical outfit, it was with the growing realization that the moment of truth was drawing rapidly closer. Those butterflies in my tummy were beginning to stir. No, I wasn't frightened. Nervous, yes – but not frightened. Nor did my nervousness arise from any concern for my ultimate survival, for at no stage did I contemplate or fear the prospect of a fatal accident. I was just worried that I might do something wrong – that I would let the Captain down by doing something quite silly. Would I remember to do all that he had told me? Would I get the landing right? Yes – I had to admit that the landing worried me. It wasn't that I minded a broken leg so much, but what a fool I would look being carried back into the grounds wearing a splint! And would Captain Gaudron then want me for his team? Oh, I knew I could do it. But could I do it *well*?

So ran my thoughts as I donned the navy-blue bloomers and the tunic with its sailor-style collar adorned with its parachute badge. A gold-coloured sash around my wait set it off nicely, and the peaked cap perched on my bushy hair gave me added height. Unfortunately the high-legged leather boots that I had ordered had not yet been delivered, so I would have to jump in ordinary shoes. I possessed a good, wasp-waisted figure but had never before been so conscious of it, accustomed as I was to the long skirts and dresses of the time. I felt very self-conscious as I made my way into the balloon enclosure, but was not entirely oblivious to nor displeased by the admiring glances that my appearance attracted, especially from the gentlemen.

Captain Gaudron had been in the enclosure since early morning attending to the filling of the balloon with domestic gas, and to the many details that an ascent of this nature necessitated. He was now busy supervising the final preparations. The magnificent golden balloon that was about to hoist me into my first aerial adventure swayed gracefully in the light breeze and tugged gently at the ropes that still held it to earth. It seemed impatient to be away – eager for the freedom of the sky. The parachute was in position, the crown attached to the netting by its piece of cocoa string, and the canopy and lines fully stretched in a graceful curve to where the trapeze bar awaited me in the basket. So limp and lazy the parachute looked now, but I had no cause to mistrust it. It would come to life when needed. Captain Gaudron would have checked it personally, and in him I had every confidence. He would not let me down. Nor, I hoped, would I let him down.

The balloon was the centre of attraction for thousands of excited onlookers, for whom the preparations were spectacles in themselves. The expectant faces completely ringed the enclosure, and from them emanated a loud hum of anticipation. Then Captain Gaudron, immaculate in his own navy-blue uniform, was calling me forward. The time had come.

The noise of the throng faded and a gradual hush descended upon the vast crowd as Captain Gaudron escorted his four passengers and me towards the basket. The principal actors were taking the stage, and I was the leading lady! I was too occupied with more basic instincts to dwell on any feelings of self-importance, however. With quickening heartbeats I took my position as instructed, perching on the rim of the basket with my feet dangling over the side. My right hand clutched the trapeze bar, whilst my left arm was wound round the ropes that connected the wicker basket to the netting of the huge monster that loomed and swayed above our heads. The passengers, with much nervous banter, positioned themselves as directed. What, I wondered, had *they* got to be nervous about?

With a last look about him to ensure that all was in order, and with a final glance in my direction – perhaps to assure himself that I was still there – the Captain gave the command

---

* *"Hands off"* was the order given when a basket was attached to the balloon. To release a gas or hot-air balloon without a basket the order was *"Let go"*.

that was to signal the start of so many adventures for me in the years to come.

"Hands ... OFF!"*

The men holding the basket released their grip, and as though by magic their faces seemed suddenly to be drifting away. There was no feeling of upward movement at all. It was as though we were standing still while the earth and all those upon it were falling gently away beneath us. What a wonderful sensation!

As soon as the balloon was set free, the silence and the tension were broken by a roar from the spectators, whose tumultuous cheers followed us into the air. To the upturned faces and to the waving of hands and hats and parasols, our passengers responded by waving their handkerchiefs from within the basket. I did not join in all this waving, I was too busy holding on.

However, the gradually increasing distance between me and *terra firma* caused me no great anxiety. Instead, I was delighted and fascinated as the landscape below began to slide slowly beneath us as though on giant rollers, and took on the aspect of a Lilliputian scene, with dolls' houses becoming smaller and smaller, and the dolls themselves dwindling to the size of scurrying ants.

The cheers and the waving faded as the majestic balloon lifted us slowing into a profound silence that was broken only by the cleek... cleek... cleek of the gently swaying basket, and the voices of its passengers filled with exhilaration and wonder. I did not join in their conversation and, indeed, was oblivious of my fellow travellers, as I was so absorbed in the dream-like quality of this experience as we drifted with the soft breeze over the tapestry of parks and streets and fields. Then knowing that the time must be approaching for me to leap from the relative security of the basket, my mind became concentrated on my descent.

What would it be like, dropping into this vast ocean of air ...those first few seconds before the parachute opened? What *would* it be like? And whereabouts down there would I land? I must remember all that the Captain had taught me... must remember to throw myself on to my back as soon as my feet hit the ground. Was it really *me* up there, perched on the edge of this floating basket, looking down on this incredible moving map? There were thousands and thousands of ordinary people down there, doing thousands of ordinary things, and here was I...

"We are over two thousand feet. Get ready to jump." The Captain's calm voice broke into my reveries. It was like a piece of ice being dropped into the pit of my stomach.

"There's a nice green field over there," he was saying, pointing outwards and downwards at what looked like a green pocket-handkerchief set amongst roads as narrow as string, and clumps of trees like pieces of moss. "Remember how to land," he reminded me, then uttered a loud: "GO!"

Gripping the trapeze bar tightly with both hands, I took a deep breath and launched myself into space...

Oh, that first fall! What a heady mixture of fright and sheer exhilaration it was ! My heart rose into my mouth as I plummeted for what seemed far too long, dropping like a stone. I could hear the rapid flap-flap-flap of the silk streaming after me as the canopy broke from the balloon netting and sucked at the rush of air, and then at last there was a big whooooosh... the sling tightened, and the trapeze bar tugged at my arms... the parachute was open!

"Thank goodness..." I was saying to myself, "...thank goodness!"

I looked up. The canopy was stretched over me like a beautiful silken dome, billowing softly as though it were breathing – as though, like me, it was glad to be alive... glad to be free. It was, at that moment, the dearest friend I had in the world. I gave it a joyful smile.

Suspended there in the clear, warm air, high above the land of mere mortals, I experienced a sense of elation such as I had never known. But the wonderment passed as, dangling beneath my gently swaying friend, I turned my attention to the scene below. I still had to land!

Just as the earth had seemed to slip away beneath us as we had ascended in the balloon basket, now it was drifting back to meet me. Gradually the fields and the houses and the trees began to assume their rightful proportions. The Captain's aim had been good, for the field that he had chosen as my landing-place was approaching, slowly at first, then appearing to pick up speed as it came closer, until with a final rush, as though trying to grab me by the legs, the grass suddenly leapt up at me. As soon as my feet touched the ground, I threw myself on to my back.

I scrambled up, removed the belt, stepped out of the sling and felt myself all over. Everything seemed to be intact. Had I really done it?

Yes, I really had! "I've done it... I've done it!" I chanted in my excitement. "No broken bones... I've done it! And I'd like to go and do it all over again!"

I looked up into the skies. There was the balloon, sailing slowly and serenely on its way, so small now. "I think you would have approved of my landing, Captain Gaudron," I laughed, then turned my attention to my faithful parachute. It was lying on the grass, fast asleep.

As I bundled it up, people appeared from all directions. They were willing and eager to help, and almost as relieved as I to find that I was in one piece. I was soon at the centre of an admiring and chattering throng.

"Isn't it dangerous?"

"Fancy a *girl* doing it!"

"Do you enjoy it?"

"I'd be scared stiff."

I tried to assume the nonchalant airs of a hardened professional. "Oh, it's nothing to fear," I replied to the barrage of questions. "It's a most wonderful sensation."

The pony and trap were soon on the spot, and my impromptu reception committee cheered me from the field as I was driven off at a smart trot. An even greater reception awaited me back at the 'Ally Pally', where the crowds who had attended our departure and had witnessed my descent from afar had stayed to applaud the return of the daring parachutist!

47

As I stood there waving to the cheering throng and shaking the hands that sought mine, I was astounded to find myself the object of such adulation. After all, I had only set out to enjoy myself!

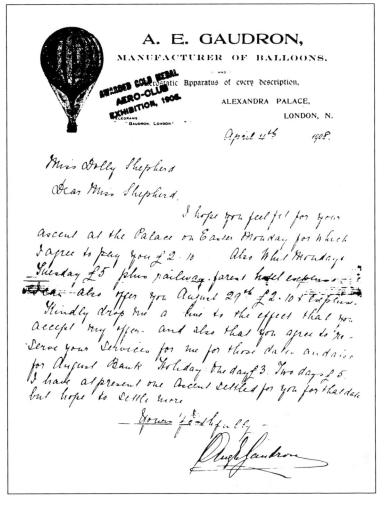

One of Captain Gaudron's letters booking me for a number of shows in 1908 and offering the usual terms. £2 10s. was a lot of money in those days!

Al: A studio portrait of myself in the attire of an Edwardian lady parachutist. My famous knickerbocker suit was very daring attire for a young lady of those times! *(p 40)*

A2: *Left* – My Aunt Mariam, proprietress of the Ostrich Feather Emporium in Holborn, was a very great influence on my early life but would have nothing to do with my parachuting activities *(p 36)*

A3: *Right* – My Uncle Will bore a striking resemblance to, and was sometimes mistaken for, King Edward! 'Mountebank stunts' he called my parachute shows. *(p 131)*

Programme of Aeronautical Displays

For EXHIBITIONS, FÊTES AND GALAS,

Conducted by A. E. GAUDRON and Staff of Competent Assistants.

1. AIRSHIP or NAVIGABLE BALLOON ASCENTS.

2. CAPTIVE BALLOON ASCENTS.
   Making ascents every 15 minutes. Taking passengers to a height of 500 or 1,000 feet.
   40,000 to 50,000 cubic feet of gas, and a steam winch required.

3. RIGHTAWAY BALLOON ASCENTS.
   Taking passengers; number according to size of Balloon used.
   From 12,000 to 60,000 cubic feet of gas required.

4. POINT-TO-POINT BALLOON RACES.
   Between 2, 3, 4 or more Balloons.
   For two Balloons 30,000 cubic feet of gas required.

5. PARACHUTE DESCENT.
   By Lady or Gentleman from a Gas Balloon.
   13,000 cubic feet of gas required.

6. PARACHUTE DESCENT.
   By Lady or Gentleman from a Hot-Air Balloon. Ascent can be made anywhere.
   No gas required.

7. DOUBLE PARACHUTE DESCENT.
   By Lady and Gentleman from Gas or Hot-Air Balloon.
   If gas, 18,000 cubic feet required.

8. RIGHTAWAY BALLOON ASCENT & PARACHUTE DESCENT.
   By a Lady from same Balloon; making two displays with one Balloon.
   28,000 cubic feet of gas required.

9. RIGHTAWAY BALLOON ASCENT & DOUBLE PARACHUTE DESCENT.
   By two Ladies or Lady and Gentleman from same Balloon; making a treble display with one Balloon.
   40,000 cubic feet of gas required.

10. SAME DISPLAY AS No. 9.
    Using two Balloons.
    50,000 to 60,000 cubic feet of gas required.

11. NIGHT PASSENGER BALLOON ASCENT.
    Carrying Fireworks and Motto.
    28,000 cubic feet of gas required.

Terms and further particulars on application to

A. E. GAUDRON, Aeronaut,
ALEXANDRA PALACE,
LONDON, N.

TELEGRAMS:
"GAUDRON, LONDON."

A4: Captain Auguste Gaudron, one of the premier aerial showmen of the Edwardian era, offered a wide choice of aerial delights in 1907.

A6: Well dressed ladies of the time. With Mrs O'Brian, with whom I used to stay on my appearances in the Wolverhampton area, and in whose husband's medical practice I used to assist as 'nurse' Shepherd. *(p 120)*

A5: *Left* – All set for 'Hands Off!' Captain Gaudron settles the passengers in the basket of the 'right-away' balloon as I, astride the sling and gripping the trapeze bar, wait to be hoisted into the air. This clearly shows the extent of my 'equipment' and the manner of ascent. Photographed in Wolverhampton in 1910. *(p 87)*

A7: At Pickering in Yorkshire the hot-air balloon is prepared for action, with the 'big mouth' positioned over the chimney of the fire trench and firmly held by Captain Gaudron's team of local volunteers, while the crowd watches with growing excitement from outside the enclosure. *(p 59)*

A8: Away we go! This was the occasion at Pickering when I was dragged through the top of the tree at the beginning of the ascent. The broken branch can be seen tangled in the parachute cords – as can the liberating cord running down the centre of the 'chute, and the sandbag. *(p 110)*

A9: Cameramen never got close enough to photograph my actual landings! Here, some of the spectators at the Pickering gala watch me descending in the distance – just above the trees at the right – with the balloon in this instance coming down more slowly than I did. *(p 111)*

At enormous expense, the Committee have arranged for a Grand

BALLOON ASCENT
AND DARING AND GRACEFUL
☙ DOUBLE ☙
☞ PARACHUTE DESCENT
BY MISS
DOLLY SHEPHERD
THE PARACHUTE QUEEN, AND
MONS. AUGUSTE E. GAUDRON

THE KING OF BALLOONISTS. (From the Alexandra Palace, London). ...ace from the Clouds (6,000 feet high) to the Earth! The most Thrilling and Sens... ...ual Feat of Modern Times.

The Grantham BOROUGH BRASS BAND

A10: A certain amount of artistic licence went into this poster, which advertised the descent at Grantham when I had a close encounter with a steam train. *(p 95)*

A11: Two other members of the Gaudron team: 'Devil-may-care Captain Smith and handsome, dashing Captain Fleet'. They both 'disappeared', as my cryptic note on Fleet's photograph suggests. The title 'Professor' was sometimes assumed by leading aeronauts of the time as an alternative to 'Captain'. *(p 66)*

Professor FLEET,

Killed

The Premier Parachutist of the World.
—*Vide Press.*

A12: Captain Gaudron – in peaked cap in right foreground – supervises the preparation of the gas balloon for a show in Wolverhampton.

④

Solo!

I was paid the sum of £2 10s. for my first public appearance as a parachutist. Captain Gaudron was well pleased. It was neither the remuneration nor the congratulations that so thrilled me that day, however. What lingered in my mind was the dream-like ascension into the skies; the exquisite excitement of the long drop from the basket; the gentle ride down under the smiling canopy; the sense of achievement as I scrambled to my feet after the landing. These were the delights that captured me. These were the pleasures that I longed to repeat. Nowadays one would say that I was well and truly 'hooked'!

My ambition for further excitement was soon fulfilled, for during the weeks that followed I made several more descents, all from the side of a basket of a 'right-away' balloon under the watchful eye of Captain Gaudron. As I gained in experience and confidence, I became more receptive to the wonderful sensations of flight and more aware of my surroundings. During the ascent – no longer lost in contemplation of my immediate future – I was able to chat to the paying passengers, and whenever we went up from the Alexandra Palace, I could point out to them some of the major features of the landscape as it spread itself below us. Looking down from my perch on the basket's edge, I was soon able to recognize and piece together all the bits of the scenic jigsaw. There was Wood Green with the Catholic church which I used to attend as a child, and Barratt's Sweet Factory so prominent, and the railway lines glinting in the sunlight, and far too many buildings to be a good place to land... Hornsey beyond, with green fields and parks... Muswell Hill to the west, and Old Southgate to the north with its familiar landmarks of childhood now seen from a completely new perspective. Across to the east lay the marshy strip of the Lee Valley, and when it was not too hazy, one could almost see Old Father Thames. And as for the 'Ally Pally' itself, receding in the distance, why – I could have put it in my pocket!

We would go where the wind took us, always hoping that it would be in the direction of Hornsey, which offered the most generous fields and open spaces. With one eye on our drift and the other on our altitude – registered by the recording of atmospheric pressure on an aneroid barometer in a large wooden case – Captain Gaudron would select a suitable landing area, and when he judged our position to be right, he would give me the signal to go. With a happy "Cheerio" to the startled passengers, I would take my leave of them. After a matter of only a few jumps, I became quite blasé about launching myself into space, although there was always, of course, that heart-throbbing moment or two waiting for the 'chute to open – but that itself was all part of the thrill. The gentle descent under the canopy was always a delightful sensation, and even the landing soon lost its menace. I was able to judge more exactly when the ground was going to hit me, and to prepare myself accordingly. I was not going to break a leg after all, I decided.

Captain Gaudron was a very astute showman, as well as a talented aeronaut, and as such he was well aware that an attractive female face and a trim figure drew more spectators to an aerial event than even the most dashing male parachutist. This was particularly so at the 'Ally Pally', where balloon ascents and even parachute descents had become a weekly occurrence during the summer months. Gaudron himself jumped every Thursday, and on one occasion had tried to enliven the proceedings by making a descent seated on a bicycle, which he prudently discarded before impact. However, he knew that the best drawing-card of all was a lady performer, and always had several of us in his team.

This was nothing new, of course. A century of aerial

showmanship had sought to attract and sustain public interest with a succession of attractive faces. After her aunt – Madame Garnerin – had made the first parachute descent by a woman, Elisa Garnerin had become one of the foremost exhibition jumpers during the period 1816 to 1836, followed by Louise Poitevin, wife of the French aeronaut Eugène Poitevin. With the renewed interest in parachuting that followed the advent of Baldwin's flexible parachute in the 1880s, daring young ladies were again in demand by the aerial impresarios. It paid to have a family connection. Van Tassel's two daughters trained as acrobats, became well known exhibition jumpers, and those showmen without parachuting daughters tended to 'adopt' one. In Britain, both Gaudron and Spencer had recruited ladies into their respective teams when they began their shows in the late 1890s. My ill-fated predecessor Maud Brooks had been one of the first, making descents as early as 1897.

As the latest recruit to this unique profession, I was soon made aware that the 'goods' had to be well displayed. It was essential that I should be seen by and should mingle with the people who came to watch. 'Showing myself' the Captain called it. It was all part of the act, and a very enjoyable part too. People would begin to gather round the enclosure several hours before the performance, to watch the preparation of the balloon and also in the hope that they might catch a glimpse of the aeronauts. I would always be well dressed in fashionable clothes for this 'showing', and would wander around the enclosure chatting to the folk on the other side of the rope and endeavouring to answer their hundreds of questions:

"Are you *really* going up in that thing?;

"What's it feel like, right up in the sky?"

"What if it didn't open?"

"Aren't you scared?"

"What would happen if you let go of the bar?"

I would try to persuade them that it was neither as frightening nor as dangerous as it might appear; that it was the most wonderful sensation in the world; that I had absolutely no intention of ever letting go of the bar! They were rarely convinced.

"Oh, but you shouldn't be doing this, a girl like you!" the older people would conclude, with a sad shake of their heads.

"I wouldn't trust myself to that," the younger ones would say.

Young boys were the most inquisitive. Their questions would be of a technical nature about the balloon and the parachute, and whenever possible I would take them into the enclosure to show them the apparatus. How they loved that!

The ladies in the crowd were more interested in me than in the equipment. In the leisurely conversations that one had time for in those less hurried days, instant friendships would blossom. I would have more invitations to tea than I could ever accept. Often I found myself no longer talking but just listening as some dear lady poured out her troubles to me or told me her life story. There was an affinity between spectators and performer that was quite unique, and when the time came for me to change into my parachuting outfit and take to the air, I would have hundreds of new friends, all of them anxious for my safety. No matter how long it took for me to be returned to the arena after I had landed in some distant field, those 'friends' would still be there to welcome me back with rapturous applause.

As soon as Captain Gaudron judged that I was proficient enough in the basic skills of parachuting as practised from the side of the basket, he declared that it was time for me to make a descent from *under* the basket of a manned balloon. This would mean that the parachute would be suspended from the underside of the basket itself during the ascent, with me already on the end of it. It would be a step towards the ultimate goal – a solo performance. I was much excited at the prospect.

The venue for this new experience was Wolverhampton where we were to appear as the major attraction at a fête on the outskirts of the city. Arriving by train, Captain Gaudron and I were met by a welcoming committee, who escorted us to our hotel and saw that we were well entertained and provided for during the evening. I decided that I rather liked this VIP treatment!

The following morning we were conveyed with our equipment to the park where the day's entertainments were to take place. In the roped-off enclosure the gas pipe was already laid out for use, and Captain Gaudron wasted no time in commencing the lengthy preparations. There was no shortage of willing helpers, for it was considered a great privilege to be part of the action inside the arena rather than a mere spectator outside it.

I watched the proceedings with interest, for if I was to become responsible for my own 'solo' balloon, I would need to know more about the means of preparing it for flight. The great envelope of varnished cotton was spread on the ground with the valve uppermost and central, and the neck pulled out to one side. Over this the net was positioned, with a few sandbags already round its circumference. The gas pipe was then connected to the neck, and the inflation began. The time that this might take depended upon the size of the balloon and the diameter of the gas pipe. With a small pipe of two and a half inches it could take all day, but with the larger four-inch pipe that we had on this occasion, three hours would suffice. Coal gas was used in preference to the hydrogen or helium necessary for high altitude or long-distance flights because it was far less expensive. What a business it must have been for the pioneers who, without recourse to coal gas, had manufactured their hydrogen through the lengthy and cumbersome process of pouring sulphuric acid on to iron filings!

Captain Gaudron watched carefully to ensure that no creases formed in the fabric as it began to swell, and that the net was kept in position and hung with ballast as required. When at last the huge bag was plump with gas, the pipe was disconnected and the balloon allowed to rise until first the suspension ring and then the basket could be attached beneath it. Finally, to the underside of the basket was fixed the parachute. Its apex was attached there by a simple cotter pin, which would be extracted by a tug on the liberating cord which ran down the inside of the canopy to the parachutist. It was essential that the canopy and lines of the 'chute, stretched to their full length on the ground, should be thoroughly checked before the ascent. Captain Gaudron showed me how to fold the silken canopy into tidy pleats and to straighten out the cords.

"If the cords become entangled," he explained, "the result would probably be fatal, so you must be extra careful to check them."

I was very careful indeed.

While all this activity was taking place, the crowds around the enclosure had increased enormously as some twenty thousand people thronged into the park to enjoy the many forms of entertainment that were on offer for this holiday occasion. I was kept busy chatting to folk from all walks of life – miners, factory hands, workers from Wolverhampton's newly founded motor car industry, people in from the country – a real mixed bag, mostly in family groups. The broad Midland vowels were strange to my ear, but the people themselves were every bit as friendly and curious and as concerned for my safety as were the Londoners of the 'Ally Pally'. People don't differ much behind their accents, I decided.

Then Captain Gaudron was calling me forward. The 'Greatest Attraction of the Fête' was about to take place.

Whilst the Captain rallied his passengers and made his final examination of the basket and the valve cord and the ripping-cord, I checked once more that the canopy and lines of my parachute ran straight and true, then stepped into the trailing sling, took a firm grip on the trapeze bar and signified that I was ready. The crowd quietened into that almost uncanny hush that always preceded an ascent. I watched the basket attentively.

"Hands... OFF!" boomed the Captain's voice.

The helpers released the basket and stepped back. It rose silently from the ground. With beating heart I tightened my grip on the bar, and as the parachute was lifted by its apex from the grass, like a rearing snake, I ran three or four steps forward to be directly beneath it and then... my feet were suddenly whisked from the ground! What a truly marvellous feeling, to be lifted into the air like that, as though by a giant and gentle hand!

The cheers of the crowd followed us into the air. Being by now bold enough to hold on to the bar with one hand, I waved my little silk Union Jack in happy response to the upturned faces. They waved and cheered the more, but the faces and the cheers soon faded from sight and sound as I was wafted away from them like a piece of thistledown.

I looked up. The cords ran in straight lines to the mouth of the canopy, and the canopy to the underside of the basket, and beyond them loomed the bulk of the balloon, dark against the blue of the sky. I could see white faces peering over the rim of the basket at me as I swung there below them, like a lazy pendulum, dangling in space. I chuckled to myself to think how nervous those passengers would be for my safety – far more nervous than I was, for there was absolutely no fear in me as I swung there. I looked down again. Between my boots and the now distant earth there was nothing. I wriggled my feet and laughed, I was walking on air... I really was *walking on air!* Oh, I felt as light and free and as gay as a butterfly!

Going *up* under a parachute, I decided, was just as wonderful as coming *down* under one. And thinking about coming down – I realized that we must by now be approaching our usual drop height of two thousand feet. I looked up again to make certain that the parachute had not become twisted during the ascent, then sure enough the Captain's distant voice was advising me to get ready, then bellowing the command to "GO!"

Twisting the liberating cord around my right hand, I gave it a good hard jerk. Instantly I was hurtling downwards. Gripping the bar with both hands I waited for that reassuring tug on the arms and the 'whooosh' of the opening canopy to tell me that my friend had woken up.

When the parachute had blossomed above me, I gave it its usual smile, then turned my attention to the landscape below. Wolverhampton itself lay sprawled untidily to one side of me, a mass of close dwellings, factories and giant steelworks. Fortunately the hundreds of chimneys were on holiday, otherwise I am sure that everything in that direction would have been obscured by smoke. To the other side of me stretched a patchwork quilt of fields and large estates. Fortunately, it was in that direction that I was being taken by the breeze, eventually to touch down safely in a freshly ploughed field.

As usual local people ran to greet me and to offer any assistance that I might need. A horse-drawn carriage soon arrived to take me in triumph back to the fête where, carrying my rolled-up parachute, I mounted the bandstand to wave to the cheering crowd.

The next step was to go solo. I could scarcely wait.

This ambition was fulfilled a few weeks later, at Ashby-de-la-Zouch.

For a solo ascent and descent there would be no basket at all. No passengers. No Captain Gaudron. Just me, my parachute and the balloon. It was a great responsibility, but I felt equal to it. I had proved to the Captain that I possessed the necessary strength, stamina and courage, and that my judgement was sound. Going solo would require all of these. I was heartened by the confidence that the Captain had in me, and I was determined not to let him down.

The advantage of a solo performance was that a much smaller balloon could be used, thus economising on gas. The balloon that I was about to use, and that I was to come to regard as my very own, had a capacity of only twenty thousand cubic feet. I watched with interest as the Captain supervised its inflation in the enclosure at Ashby.

It was a hot day, with not a cloud in the bright blue sky. I looked up into it. Soon it would be all mine. I would be the sole occupant of that blue ocean. I felt a thrill of anticipation wriggle through me.

There was the usual sense of excitement as the balloon took shape. After I had checked my parachute and the release mechanism that attached it to the suspension ring below the balloon, Captain Gaudron gave me my final instructions and reminded me of the most important points:

"Do not go too high. Gauge the direction and force of the wind before deciding to pull away. Select your landing-ground away from houses and other obstructions. And above all remember – if you are twisted around under the balloon, you must wait until you unwind before you pull away. *Bon voyage*," he concluded.

The small balloon was then allowed to rise until the ring, to which the netting that covered the bag was attached, was being held at arm's length by the men waiting for the signal to release it. This time it was I who would give the order. I stepped into the sling and took up the trapeze bar.

"LET GO!" I cried, in a firm voice.

Up went the balloon, and away I sailed beneath it, waving my little flag as I went. Up and up and up I soared, leaving behind the cheers and the faces and the waving hats, rising rapidly into a world of utter and incredible silence. The sounds of the crowd, the barking of dogs, and the songs of the birds were lost, for with increasing height all nature becomes silent. Nor is the stillness of a balloon ascent broken by the sound of the wind, for the balloon becomes *part* of that wind. It moves with it. It belongs to it. There was not even the creaking of the basket or the muffled voices of its occupants that had accompanied my previous ascents. I was alone. Alone in the immensity of the sky. Alone in its silence.

Yet I was not frightened. On the contrary I was enthralled. Whilst I felt so tiny in the vast expanse of the sky, I could not help but experience at the same time a sense of importance at being its only occupant. There was not a cloud or a bird to share it with. I was too high for the birds. There was just me and my friend the parachute, and our balloon lifting us higher and higher into the blue... into the silence.

"No one, but *no one* can imagine what this is like!" I said to them, but they didn't answer.

As I looked up at them, my eye caught sight of the small personal aneroid that I wore on the inside of my wrist to advise me of my altitude. Over two thousand feet already! So entranced had I been by the ecstasy of silence that I had lost account of height and time. I looked downwards, in the direction in which we were travelling. There was an ample choice of fields, and no serious or obvious obstructions in view.

"Here goes..." I said aloud to the silence, and gave an almighty tug on the ripping-cord that simultaneously released the parachute and ripped the valve of the balloon open. There was the now familiar drop of some 250 feet before the canopy opened and slowed my fall. A moment later I was startled by a hissing, flapping noise. Relieved of my weight, the balloon had been unceremoniously turned upside down by the heavy sandbag attached to the upper netting for that very purpose, allowing the gas to escape through the neck. It was the sound of the deflating bag rushing earthwards that I now heard. The poor balloon – it sounded most unhappy as it wheezed and flapped its way to the ground. I too would have liked to have prolonged our aerial voyage.

"We'll go higher next time!" I called after it.

Hoping for a soft landing, I enjoyed as always the gentle, swaying descent under the big silk umbrella. Within minutes I was picking myself up from the corner of a field. As I bundled my parachute, I was conscious of the songs of the birds, which for a short while I had left far behind me.

My apprenticeship was not yet fully served. Having mastered solo descents from a gas balloon, I still had to experience a descent from the hot-air variety. Hot-air was used on those occasions when a supply of gas was either inadequate or unavailable. The filling of a balloon was in theory a straightforward process but was in fact an operation that required great skill and judgement.

My introduction to this novel form of transportation was to take place at Pickering, in Yorkshire. During the long but pleasant train journey from London, Captain Gaudron had ample time to explain to me how the balloon would be prepared and operated, and the actions that I would need to take. He emphasised the importance of timing: timing of the ascent to coincide with maximum lifting power, and timing of the descent to ensure that lifting power was not lost through the cooling of the air inside the bag. Too little lift and there would be insufficient height for the parachutist to drop. Go too high before pulling away, and the air might cool, causing the balloon to deflate and collapse on top of the parachutist – which would be fatal. It all sounded very exciting.

We were, as usual, met at the station by members of the fête committee, who entertained us to an excellent dinner and installed us in one of the finest hotels in this charming market town.

The day of my first hot-air ascent dawned fair, with a cloudless sky. When I went down to breakfast, I learnt that the Captain had already left the hotel for the fête grounds. What a conscientious and hard-working man he was – attributes for which I was most grateful, for my very life depended upon them. Within the hour I too set off, fashionably dressed in a sage-blue costume with long skirt and short train, broad brimmed hat trimmed with flowers, and blue gloves, and carrying a handbag to match.

Once at the grounds I made straight for the balloon enclosure, which was already a scene of great activity. Under Captain Gaudron's direction, shirtsleeved volunteers were energetically digging a trench some three feet deep and fifty feet long, while others were unloading a good quantity of wood and straw from a cart. The balloon lay like a huge, inert sack at one end of the trench. It was rather an ugly-looking creature, made of thicker fabric than the gas balloons to which I had become accustomed. There was no net, no valve and a much wider opening at its base – called the 'big mouth'. Running round the whole of this mouth and threaded through metal rings was a wire rope, which would be pulled to close the balloon when it had taken its fill of hot air.

When the trench was completed to the Captain's satisfaction, it was filled with timber and straw, then covered with sheets of corrugated iron, which in turn were covered with earth, leaving an opening at the up-wind end, and a small chimney at the other. On either side of this outlet were erected tall poles, and by means of a pulley the huge bag was hoisted between them, with its mouth poised over the chimney. I could hardly believe that this inert creature was going to carry me into that lovely blue sky above our heads.

Whilst all this was going on, I took the opportunity to check my parachute, already stretched out on the ground a safe distance from the fire trench. It was late morning by the time the preparations were completed, and people were already arriving at the grounds. By noon they were pouring in by the hundreds, and my duties began. Strolling round the perimeter of the enclosure. I was soon chatting lightheartedly to those on the outside, constantly shaking hands, signing autographs for small boys and girls, answering the now familiar questions and exchanging experiences of life in general with the grown-ups.

There was a loud buzz of excitement when the fire was lit at the end of the trench. In a few minutes smoke was pouring from the chimney, to be gulped up hungrily by the 'big mouth'. Some of the smoke escaped, to drift over the crowd on the down-wind side of the arena. With exclamations and much good-natured laughter they hurriedly dispersed to better vantage points. A group of helpers were already holding the rope to keep the mouth open and to prevent the balloon from rising prematurely as it filled with hot air. Captain Gaudron's experienced eye monitored the whole procedure.

As the great bag began to show signs of life, it was time for me to change. When I reappeared, the balloon was almost fully inflated. I again made a tour of the arena, adding to the mounting excitement and warmed as always by the friendliness that reached out to me from the spectators.

There was a loud "Ahhhhh..." as the supporting poles and the pulley were dismantled, leaving the balloon to stand there by itself, puffed out with pride now, as though saying "You see – I don't need those silly poles!"

The Captain was attaching the crown of the parachute to the release device at the mouth of the balloon. I cast a final glance over the stretched-out canopy and cords, then stepped into the sling and took hold of the bar.

"Remember," called the Captain, "Take no chances – you must pull away at fifteen hundred."

I nodded and eyed the 'big mouth' expectantly. It required ten pairs of hands to hold it down now as it tugged and strained like some monster eager for its freedom. Tension mounted. The wire rope was pulled tight through the rings and quickly secured. The crowd fell silent.

"LET GO!" roared the Captain.

Thankfully, the crew let go. Equally relieved, the balloon headed for the sky, dragging me after it. In answer to the jubilant cheers, I waved my little flag as I was borne aloft, swinging beneath my bag of hot air. The sensation was much the same as that of an ascent under the gas balloon, apart from the smell of smoke that lingered in my nostrils, like the childhood scent of bonfires in my father's beloved garden.

The crowd and the park and the town itself dwindled, and there was the broad sweep of moorland rolling away to the north, and the verdant pastures of the Vale of Pickering to the south. I had little time to admire the scenic grandeur, however, for I knew how important it was for me to part company with my hot-air friend before his enthusiasm cooled and he collapsed on top of me. At the same time, I had to be high enough to give my parachute ample time to open fully. The Captain's words hammered in my brain: "Take no chances – you must pull away at fifteen hundred." So my attention was occupied more by my aneroid than by the scenery.

As I neared the crucial height, I looked below for a suitable landing spot. "There – that beautiful piece of green velvet will do," I said to myself, and gave a hard pull on the ripping cord. Away we went, my parachute and I, leaving the poor balloon to wonder what was happening as the sandbag tied to its crown promptly turned it upside down, spilling out its hot air in a great belch of black smoke. Swinging beneath the opened canopy, I watched it make its ungainly way back to earth. I was very grateful to it, of course, but decided that I preferred my little gas balloon. Somehow it was more elegant. I could also go higher in a gas balloon – as high as I liked. Little did I realize, as I mused on the pleasures of altitude, that the day would come when I would experience an almost fatal surfeit of it...

My judgement had been sound, for I landed squarely and safely in the field that only minutes before had been my piece of green velvet. Soon I was being conveyed back to the arena and the acclaim of my 'friends'.

I was now an accomplished solo parachutist – a fully qualified member of the Gaudron team.

And who, I had often asked myself, were the other members of this team to which I now belonged? Our leader was a dynamic and warm-hearted person, and a gentleman in the full sense of the word. It was not difficult for a man of such charisma and experience to gather round him a group of individuals all imbued with the same sense of adventure and love of the air. At any one time there were usually about eight of us in the team, but rarely did we see each other, for we worked singly or in pairs according to the commitments entered into with the Captain. The requests to make a descent would come to us direct from Monsieur Gaudron himself, written in his wife's fair hand, with none of the flourishes associated with the French.

Viola Kavanah was one of my closest associates within the team. She was a vivacious girl, always happy. For her, aeronautics was almost a full-time job. She worked not only for Gaudron but also for the Spencers, often under a different name and even on occasions as 'Elsa Spencer'. We enjoyed several performances together, and Viola was always ready to stand in for any one of us who for some reason or other was unable to keep a parachuting appointment. Poor Viola – she was to stand in once too often...

Then there was Flo Lusby, a well-built girl, always full of fun. Flo and I were amongst the few female parachutists to survive those pioneering years.

The men I knew less well, as it was Captain Gaudron himself who usually accompanied me on my performances.

Eames, Taylor, Hickes, Smith, Fleet – adventurers, all of them.
Splendid men. In addition to being first-class parachutists, they
were also qualified to pilot 'right-away' balloons and as such
were usually styled 'Captain', a title with no military significance but one that was traditionally adopted by aeronauts
of stature. They were true professionals, those men.

During the whole eight years that I worked for Gaudron,
the only time that we met as a complete team was not at a
showground but at Euston Station! It was on a Sunday, which
was the day of the week on which touring theatrical companies
moved themselves and their skips full of props around the
country. The scene at Euston was therefore a lively one, with a
milling crowd of theatre folk laughing, cajoling and shouting
in competition with the hissing of steam and swirling puffs of
smoke as trains came and went. A handful of ordinary passengers added to the confusion and hubbub as they sought
desperately to locate their trains.

I was due to travel north with Captain Gaudron for an
appearance at Stafford. Those journeys to different parts of the
country were adventures in themselves, and Monsieur Gaudron
was always a charming and interesting companion, with his
tales of the past and his visions for the future. On this occasion,
as I pushed my way through the crush of people and luggage in
my endeavours to locate him, I spied a balloon basket and made
my way towards it. The figure beside it was not Gaudron,
however – it was Captain Fleet. No mistaking him, with his
fair hair, and so tall and slim! Then I saw two more baskets –
and Captain Gaudron. He laughed at my surprise. "Yes – we
are all travelling today, but to different parts of the country!"

So it was that we all met for the first and only time, for a
brief exchange of news and good-hearted banter before the
porters were hailed to transport the heavy baskets packed with
folded balloons and tackle. With cheery cries of "Good luck"
and "Happy landings", four pairs of aeronauts zigzagged their
way through the theatrical throngs to their respective trains.

The fun was not yet over. As my companion and I settled
into our corner seats and looked out on to the still busy platform,

there was an important announcement. A strong voice boomed out: "Will George Edwards' number two company change to the train opposite." A pause. "Walter Melville's company should alight and wait further instructions." Pause. "Hurry along, please. Passengers should take their seats as the trains are about to leave."

For the next five minutes panic reigned as bodies hurled themselves from one train to another and porters were driven mad, not knowing what was happening. Pandemonium increased until someone noticed an unpretentious gent sitting quietly and unperturbed on his skip. It was none other than a ventriloquist practising his art and his sense of humour on his fellows! There was an explosive uproar before the theatrical world recovered its equilibrium and scrambled back into its original trains with only a few minutes to spare!

We had a lot in common with the theatrical profession. We also were showmen, and like them we aeronauts lived by the principle that 'the show must go on'. If any of the team was unable to fulfil a particular engagement, there was always someone willing to step in and take his or her place.

It happened to me once – rather unexpectedly. I had gone to the Alexandra Palace to watch one of my male colleagues make a descent from a hot-air balloon. It was a pleasant summer day, and I mingled with the crowd, quite content to be no more than a spectator for a change. In the arena were all the signs of imminent departure. The balloon was full and tugging impatiently at the hand of those who held it. The parachute was already attached and laid out on the ground. There was one thing missing: the parachutist.

Captain Gaudron stood there with an agitated look on his face. The crowd began to realize that something was wrong, and hushed as the Captain made an announcement. Apologetically he explained that his parachutist had not yet arrived and that the performance would have to be delayed. There was a groan of disappointment from the assembly. Several, however, had recognized me as I had strolled amongst them, and faces were now turning towards me, and voices were calling out, "Dolly Shepherd's here... Dolly Shepherd's here."

I knew how critical it was for the ascent to take place before the air in the balloon cooled. Soon it would be too late, and there would be no show at all. I made my way into the enclosure.

"Hello, Captain Gaudron," I said. "Don't worry – I'll go up."

"But you have no uniform," he observed.

"Never mind about that. I'll go as I am," I said, and turning to the crowd I called out, "Has anyone a large safety pin?"

A pin was produced. Drawing my billowy, full-length skirt between my legs, I pinned it to my waist much in the fashion of some vision from an eastern harem. Off came my hat, and with a length of ribbon also borrowed from a nearby spectator I tied back my long hair. Thus attired, and wearing my high-heeled shoes, I declared myself ready for the ascent.

Captain Gaudron was much relieved. An improperly dressed parachutist was obviously better than no parachutist at all! The final checks were made, and within a few minutes I was waving happily as the hot-air balloon lifted me above the distinctive towers of the Palace and away from the tumultuous cheers of the crowd.

"Well, this *is* a surprise," I said aloud to myself as I surveyed the now familiar landscape drifting serenely beneath me. "You never know what's round the corner."

Poor Viola Kavanah – she certainly didn't know what was round the corner on the last occasion that she stood in for me. I was due to make a descent at Coventry, and when I was prevented from doing so, Viola happily took my place. She was making a perfect descent when the wind blew her from her chosen landing area and pitched her on to the high roof of a factory. There she clung for a moment, but before she could be rescued, another gust of wind caught her parachute. She was dragged from her perilous perch to fall and die on the street below.

This marvellous aerial game that I was playing was not without its hazards.

⑤

Hazards of the Air

From time to time a member of our team might 'disappear'. Nothing would be said. He or she would just not be seen at any more shows, and if questioned, Captain Gaudron would merely say that the aeronaut in question had 'left the team'. They had left, sure enough!

So Maud Brooks had 'disappeared', and Viola Kavanah. Devil-may-care Captain Smith and handsome, dashing Captain Fleet – they 'disappeared' too.

We learnt not to question these departures, for death was a subject on which we did not dwell. We might read of such an event in a newspaper, but if we did, our reaction was that of most people who flirt with danger: it might happen to them but never to *me*.

When a parachutist was involved in a serious or fatal accident there was usually a local outcry against shows of this nature, and the fête committees in that area would steer clear of these 'sensational and degrading exhibitions' until the fuss had died down. Fortunately it didn't happen often, but there is no doubt that there were dangers as well as thrills in our defiance of gravity. Indeed, had there not been, would people have flocked to see us as they did? And would we ourselves have found it so exciting?

The most serious and potentially fatal risk, of course, was that the parachute itself would not function correctly. Fortunately this was an improbable and rare occurrence, for the type of 'chute that we used – based on the Baldwin model

– was such a simple device that little could go wrong with it. Suspended at full stretch from its attachment point, there were none of the complications of deployment from a pack, and no danger of the canopy becoming entangled with the cords. Released in still air, there was also none of the 'opening shock' that one gets when jumping from a moving aircraft or after a prolonged free fall, so the parachute itself was not subjected to undue stresses and strains. The only real danger – and one that Captain Gaudron was constantly reminding me of – was of the cords or canopy becoming twisted in some way that might restrict the mouth of the 'chute, and thus prevent it from taking in air when released from its attachment point. One always experienced a certain amount of movement when suspended either from the basket or directly beneath a solo balloon. Usually it was no more than the gentle pendulum-like motion that I always found so pleasant, but if the air was at all turbulent – 'air pockets' and 'whirlwinds' we used to talk of then – one could be swung round slowly on the end of the cords. The balloon itself was also liable to revolve gently during an ascent. Because of this we not only checked the cords and canopy carefully before going up, but also had another good look at them before pulling away to make sure that they ran free and untangled to their attachment point. If they were twisted in any way, then it was a case of waiting patiently until they unwound. There was only one occasion when perhaps I didn't carry out this aerial check as thoroughly as I should have done...

It was a routine solo performance in the Midlands. The day was fine, with no more than a gentle breeze: one of the those days, you might think, when *nothing* could possibly go wrong. The release of the balloon and the ascent caused the customary excitement. To provide a spectacular display – and because I always did like to go as high as possible in any case – I let my little gas balloon take me to an altitude of over five thousand feet. It was a gentle and enjoyable ride, and I was not conscious of being turned at all as I drifted skywards, suspended happily beneath the silvery orb. Nor did I notice anything untoward when I looked up for a final visual check of the parachute extended above me.

Having selected a likely landing ground, I pulled the ripping-cord, and down I went, dropping like a stone for that now customary fall of some 250 feet, waiting for the canopy to open with its friendly exclamation. To my horror, I just kept falling.

I looked up. The cords and the canopy were streaming above me, the silk rippling and shaking as though it were desperately trying to take a deep breath of life-giving air – but its mouth remained obstinately closed. There was just enough support from the streaming parachute to keep me in an upright position as I plummeted earthwards. The only physical sensation as I fell through the air was of a strange buffeting. I felt so helpless... unable to do anything, I really did think that my time had come, and as I sped towards the ground, thoughts of the inevitable flashed through my mind. What would it feel like, to be killed? Would I feel anything at all?

I was conscious of the ground coming closer, seeming to gather speed for the blow. I felt quite numb... trees rushed up round me... this was it, I thought...

Suddenly there was a 'whooosh' above me. There was the tug of the cords on the trapeze bar. At the very moment that my plunge towards the ground was slowed by the long-overdue opening of the canopy, I hit the earth with a thud that shook every bone in my body and quite knocked the breath from me.

I lay there on my back, looking up at the blue sky through which I had just hurtled, scarcely able to believe that I was still alive – that the 'chute had opened at the very last moment. Before I could pick myself up, a masculine voice commanded, "Here, drink this," and the gentleman leaning over me produced a flask of brandy from his hip pocket. I was not usually given to drinking spirits, but sitting up, I too the flash thankfully and drained it without a word.

"I suppose you had come to pick up the pieces?" I eventually gasped.

"Well, I must admit that I didn't expect to find you in one

piece," he said.

I rose rather shakily to my feet and looked ruefully at my parachute, now lying limp on the ground. What a shock it had given me! But I couldn't be angry with it: on the contrary, I was so grateful that it had managed to take that big breath of air just in the nick of time. Its failure to open immediately could only have been due to some constriction of the canopy mouth, probably caused by the lines or the canopy itself being twisted.

The Captain was soon on the spot, amazed and absolutely overjoyed to find me on my feet and not crumpled lifeless on the ground as he had fully expected. He and the thousands of spectators at the fête had watched in horror as I had plummeted from the balloon beneath the flailing strip of silk, to disappear behind the trees which had screened from their sight the timely opening of the parachute. He was so sure that I would – at best – be seriously injured that he had brought a doctor with him. A cursory examination there and then indicated that nothing was broken, although he pronounced that I was thoroughly shaken and suffering from slight shock – which was hardly surprising, for I had come within a whisker of death.

The Captain organized the collection of my parachute, together with the balloon which had followed me down at a more sedate pace to land close by. He and the doctor then escorted me back to the fête grounds where I greeted the spectators and let them see that I was very much alive. I am sure that there were many amongst them who thought it was all part of the show, to delay the opening of the parachute until out of sight. I hoped that they would not expect a repeat performance.

I was also examined by another incredulous doctor who was a spectator at the fête, and he confirmed that I was in good physical condition, although he warned me that I would be black and blue all over by the following morning. I was, too! What amazed the doctors in this case was not just that I had survived the impact of the landing. They were even more surprised that I had survived the fall itself, for it was a commonly held belief amongst medical men and aeronauts at that time that a person falling at speed through the air would lose consciousness, if not life itself. In these modern skydiving days we know better, of course, but in 1906 the doctors shook their heads in disbelief to hear that I had fallen for almost five thousand feet with no apparent ill effect. I like to think that my unintentional 'free fall' might have done something to dispel that particular myth.

I experienced one other unplanned 'free fall', although fortunately it was of a much shorter duration. Indeed, it was an unhappy occasion for Captain Gaudron as well as for me.

We were to make a double descent from a 'right-away' balloon, to be piloted by Captain Eames at the end of August 1910. The venue was Coalville, on the outskirts of Leicester, and the two men had gone on in advance as I was unable to leave London until the last moment. The fête was in full swing when I arrived, and all was ready for the 'main attraction' of the day. The balloon was fully inflated and tugging at its bonds in a freshening wind. The basket was attached, and the two parachutes were in position, mine fastened to the underside of it, and the other suspended from the balloon for Captain Gaudron's leap from the basket itself. A cheer went up from the immense crowd as I appeared, already dressed in my smart knickerbocker suit. The Captain was also pleased to see me, knowing that now his team was complete.

Time was short, but I did not want to disappoint the public, who always liked to see me amongst them, so I asked the Captain if I had time to go and chat with them.

"Yes," he replied, "but not for long. We shall have to start in ten minutes."

I quickly walked round the enclosure, shaking the many outstretched hands, exchanging greetings and responding happily to the many good wishes.

"I'll be back with you soon," I called out as I made my way to the balloon with a wave of the hand. I was gong to be back sooner than I expected...

The tension mounted. While Captain Eames was taking his place in the basket, I cast a quick glance over my parachute. There was no time to inspect it as thoroughly as I normally would.

"This is the first time I have ever gone up without examining each cord," I said to Captain Gaudron, "I hope all will be well."

He assured me that there was no reason to worry. "But don't go too high before pulling away in this wind," he said, "I shall follow quickly after you."

He made his way to the basket and perched himself on the side of it, while I took up my stance on the ground, legs astride the sling and hands firmly gripping the trapeze bar.

"Hands... OFF!" commanded Captain Eames, and those holding the balloon stood back. The basket rose, the balloon already moving sideways as well as upwards as the wind took it. I ran forward, to be whisked swiftly and smoothly into the air, accompanied by the cheers of the crowd. As I swung out above them, their cheering turned suddenly to cries of horror, which, I vaguely realized, had something to do with me, for I was aware of quite a new sensation. Instead of soaring skywards, I was dropping back to earth, with no apparent means of support even though I was still clinging desperately to the trapeze bar. I had a blurred impression of startled, upturned faces rushing towards me. Then I went into them with a tremendous thud.

I crashed to the ground amongst the bodies that had broken my fall. There was a moment of stunned silence, then the crowd was pressing in to where I had fallen, and I could hear cries of "Is she hurt?", "Is she alive?" coming from different parts of the arena.

I rose to my feet and assured those nearest to me that I was all right, although a little shaken, and the news was quickly relayed to those further back in the crowd. "Yes, she's all right... she's all right," I could hear them calling.

I looked around me. "But what about the others?" I asked with some concern, for I had landed on them with an awful thump. "Did I injure anyone when I fell?"

"No – we're all right," said one lady – and promptly fainted. Whilst medical help was being summoned, I briefly examined the trapeze bar that I still clutched in my hands. Short lengths of cord trailed from it, but nothing else. I looked up into the sky, and now located the balloon. It was still gaining altitude and had been carried some distance from the showground by the fresh wind, but I could make out the parachute canopy and the remnants of the cords dangling freely beneath the basket. Somehow, all the cords had broken, to send me hurtling to the ground. How on *earth* could that have happened? Surely they would only have severed like that if they had been partially cut beforehand?

My thoughts were interrupted by the arrival of medical assistance. The dear lady – Mrs Bolton, wife of a local butcher – and I were taken to the first-aid tent where we were given the traditional treatment for shock – plenty of hot, sweet tea. Once again I had escaped with no more than the promise of bruises for the following day.

Members of the Committee had fought their way to the first-aid post to see if I was all right, and to ask what had happened. "We saw you rise as usual, and you were well above the heads of the crowd when suddenly you dropped like a stone. We just couldn't believe our eyes."

"I just can't imagine what went wrong," I replied. "I just don't know. But I *do* know that if my fall hadn't been broken by the crowd, or if I had gone any higher, I should not be talking to you now."

I said nothing about the broken cords, for I knew that as soon as Captain Gaudron returned from his descent, we could investigate the mystery together.

Time passed, however, and there was no Captain Gaudron. I became fearful for his safety. His parachute had been seen to open in the distance and had appeared to be carrying him down all right, so the cords of *his* 'chute had not parted. I was at least thankful for that, for had they broken at that height, nothing could have saved him. But where was he?

Just then a message arrived to say that Gaudron had had an accident but was being given treatment and would return to the showground as soon as possible. So at least he was alive, but what sort of accident was it? What had happened? It must have been something serious to have detained him for so long. We waited patiently for over an hour, wondering what could have happened to him.

When at last he did arrive, what a sight he was! He had one arm in a sling, one eye and his head swathed in bandages, and his face and neck criss-crossed with dressings. I immediately forgot my own bruises. The doctor who had accompanied the Captain back to the showground was most concerned for his welfare. He had tried to persuade him that he should stay in hospital for at least a couple of days and that he was certainly not fit to travel, but the Captain was adamant that he should get home to his wife.

"She will be worrying about me, and I *must* return to her – but I should like to send a telegram to warn her," he said, then turned his one good eye on me. "Now, what happened to you, Miss Shepherd? I was horrified to see you fall. I am so glad you are not injured."

My problems seemed insignificant compared to his, so I assured him that I was all right. "I'll tell you about it on the train," I said. "But how did *you* get so badly injured?"

Captain Gaudron explained how he had jumped from the basket at four thousand feet and had been making a normal descent until he was about to land in his chosen field. At that point the gusty wind had taken control and had dashed against a flint wall. Because of the wind on that day, he had taken the unusual precaution of wearing the belt, which had anchored him to the parachute so that he was unable to release himself quickly. When another gust filled the canopy like a billowing sail, he had been dragged over one flint wall and blown into another. By the time that he had finally managed to release himself, he had been badly knocked about, and found that he was unable to see properly. In a state of collapse he had lain there on the ground until help had arrived. Fortunately a doctor had soon been on the spot and had been able to replace the Captain's eye which had been knocked from its socket.

In response to our exclamation of horror, the Captain

assured us that it was all right, and that he had been advised by the doctor that his sight would not be impaired, provided that the eye was protected. He would, he said, be quite better after a rest at home.

"But I do not want another descent like that one," he concluded.

We commiserated with him, but he shrugged off his own problems and expressed his gratitude for the care and attention that we had both been given, and his regret that the people at the fête had not been able to enjoy the thrill of a successful performance. I thought that there might have been thrills enough for them in our *un*successful performance, and the Chairman of the Committee hastened to reassure the Captain.

"I know that you risk your life every time that you ascend, but today you *both* could have been killed. So I am glad that it is nothing worse," he said.

We were thanked for taking our mishaps so lightly and were transported to our lodgings, from which, after a rest, we were conveyed to the station and settled as comfortably in our carriage as possible for the return journey to London. What a sorry pair we looked!

As the train got under way, I explained to Captain Gaudron what had happened to me, and voiced my suspicions that the parachute cords had been partly severed before the ascent. Had he been his normal self, I am sure that he would have carried out a thorough investigation of the affair, but he was obviously in great physical distress and still in a state of shock as he reclined opposite me, so I did not press the matter further. Captain Eames would be making his own arrangements to return the balloon and the damaged parachute, so there would be no early opportunity for me to discuss the accident with him. I decided therefore to let the matter drop, and who or what might have cut or damaged those cords, and how, has remained a mystery to me every since. What I did do was to vow never to go up again without checking every single cord myself!

At the London terminus I put Captain Gaudron into a 'growler' (a four-wheeled horse-drawn cab) and asked the driver to see him home, where his wife was waiting to give him the care and attention he so badly needed. I then hurried to my aunt's house, where the housekeeper was anxiously awaiting me.

As so often happens, there was an amusing sequel to this unfortunate event. Aunty was holidaying with my mother in Great Yarmouth, which was just as well, for she knew nothing about this particular descent, and I would have found it difficult to explain my late home-coming. I was to join them the following day, so I had only a few hours' sleep before I found myself once more on a train, settling wearily and gingerly into a corner seat. I was, of course, a mass of bruises!

When I arrived at Great Yarmouth, I made my painful way to the boarding-house where my mother and aunt were staying. They greeted me cheerfully, and as we sat and chatted, Aunty – who had a tremendous sense of humour – recounted an amusing incident.

"We went shopping yesterday," she said, "for some very necessary articles – they don't provide everything in this establishment! You'll never guess what happened! We were returning in our open landau, and I was in my cream shantung outfit and best feather hat and boa. We stopped for a while at the bandstand to listen to the music – quite enchanting it was too – and when the man came round with the collecting box, I leant forward gracefully, and as I dropped the coins into the box, I must have touched the door handle. The door flew open and oh! Out rolled two packs of toilet paper and a chamber-pot – in front of all those people! Someone in the crowd returned them to us, and we hurried away at a gallop. What an embarrassment!"

She sat back and rocked all of her thirteen stone with laughter, at the same time patting me heavily on the lap and grasping me by the arm. Coo – how I winced! I tried desperately hard not to let them see how it hurt. Fortunately, rescue was at hand.

"We've been so busy this morning," my mother said, "that we haven't even had time to look at the paper."

"I'll get it," I offered, anxious to escape from Aunty's grip. I got up to fetch the newspaper from the table and as I picked it up, I glanced at the headlines. My heart skipped a beat.

"PARACHUTISTS ESCAPE – DOLLY SHEPHERD NARROWLY MISSES DEATH. CAPTAIN GAUDRON SERIOUSLY INJURED."

"It's cold in here," I said. "I think you should have a fire." Before they could object, I removed the front page of the paper, crumpled it in the grate, and proceeded to light a fire with the offending article.

My aunt never did find out about that particular escapade! Unintentional 'free fall' was not the only aerial hazard that I encountered during my career as a parachutist. On another occasion I came very close to death through not being able to fall at all!

Again the venue was Coalville – not my luckiest of show-grounds. The occasion was a Bank Holiday fête, where I was to make a descent from my little solo balloon, assisted as usual by Captain Gaudron.

The weather was fine, and whilst the Captain – with no lack of willing hands to help him – prepared the balloon, I was busy 'showing myself' to the friendly onlookers. The questions came thick and fast as I wandered around the perimeter of the enclosure.

"Where is the balloon that you are going up in?" asked one little boy shyly, holding tightly to his mother's hand.

"Over there," I replied, pointing to the semi-inflated bag rising and falling gently on the grass as it breathed in the coal gas from the pipe. "It looks a funny shape now, doesn't it?"

"It's like a sleepy animal waking up," observed the lad. "Will it really turn into a proper balloon?"

"Oh yes, your sleepy animal will turn into the most beautiful balloon you have ever seen."

Letting go of his mother's hand as he gained confidence in me, he looked intently from the growing balloon up into my face. "Are you really going up in that sleepy balloon?" he asked.

"Well," I laughed. "Not exactly *in* it, but underneath it,

attached to that parachute that you can see stretched out on the grass."

"And will that wake up as well?" he asked.

" I jolly well hope so!" I laughed.

The boy's mother then asked, "How long will it take you to go up and come down?"

"Oh, about five or six minutes to go up, and about four minutes to come down."

"And how high will you go?" queried a masculine voice.

"On a clear day like this, probably four thousand feet," I replied. How wrong I was...

So I lingered and chatted with the spectators until the balloon had taken shape and was becoming restive. The Captain signalled that departure time was approaching, so I waved goodbye to my new-found friends and turned my thoughts to the serious business of the day.

Methodically I checked each silken fold of the parachute as it lay stretched out on the grass, and examined each cord. Equally carefully Captain Gaudron attached the crown of the 'chute to the balloon.

The display was programmed for six-thirty, and right on time I took my place. As silence fell on the crowd and all eyes settled on me, I gave the order, and the men holding the balloon let go. So gracefully did it rise, and so effortlessly did it sweep me from the ground! It was a sensation that never failed to delight me. I waved my Union Jack in reply to the tumultuous cheers, and smiled down on the sea of upturned faces. Suddenly a small figure ran into the enclosure below me, followed by that of a woman in close pursuit.

"My little boy – bless him!" I laughed aloud and gave him a special wave.

The figures lost their individuality as up and up I went. It was one of those incredibly clear and sunny evenings so often experienced at that time of year, with hardly a breath of wind. Swaying gently beneath my big silvery companion, I savoured those precious moments of inexplicable joy, alone in the silence of the sky, with the beautiful tapestry spreading itself out for me to view. Buildings became as dolls' houses and fields as different coloured patches on a vast quilt. All too soon the time came to reverse the procedure – to drift back to earth just as pleasantly as I had drifted from it. The aneroid on my wrist said that I was almost at four thousand feet, and one of the patches on the quilt below seemed ideally placed to receive me, so I reached for the ripping-cord. I gave it its usual hard tug.

Nothing happened.

I pulled again. Still nothing. Again... and again... still no response. Still I swung there at the end of my unopened parachute, suspended from the balloon as it continued on its skyward journey, seemingly quite oblivious of my little problem.

"Am I dreaming?" I said aloud, and gave another tug with all my force. Nothing. I felt panic welling inside me. But that wouldn't do... I mustn't panic. Above all, I mustn't panic...

"Begin again," I told myself sternly.

I put my right hand back on the bar. Then with bated breath I stretched it out again, took the ripping-cord, wrapped it round my hand and gave an almighty jerk. Nothing. I looked up beyond my lifeless parachute to the balloon.

"Now what do I do?" I asked it.

It ignored me. It just continued to rise in its usual leisurely manner, altogether disregarding the fact that by now we should have parted company – that we should be making our separate ways back to earth. It seemed absolutely unimpressed by my predicament.

I gave yet another tug, but it was no use. The pin must have become jammed tight in the release mechanism. If I couldn't get loose, there was only one thing I could do, and that was to hang on until the balloon got tired and came down. I knew that the gas would start to escape through the neck of the bag as we went higher, and that the balloon would slowly descend. All I had to do was hang on until then.

I looked up at the balloon again. My tummy somersaulted. For a moment I felt sick. To my horror, the flap had blown inside the neck of the balloon, virtually sealing it. Would any gas be *able* to escape? Would I *ever* come down?

My heart dropped, and for a few moments I slumped there, my mind a blank. But this wouldn't do. I *couldn't* give up. I *had* to hang on. When I regained control of myself, I began to think constructively. With the sling to take most of the weight of my body, I resolved that I could stay there just as long as it would take for the balloon to tire of this silly game and return us both to earth.

Resigned to the situation, and with renewed determination, I looked again at the ground. The dolls' houses and patchwork quilt had faded into one blurred mass, and I could no longer make out the showground from which I had ascended with such confidence only a short while ago. Captain Gaudron – he would realize by now that something had gone wrong. He would have sent someone to follow me along one of those roads that now looked as thin as cotton. Could they still see me, I wondered. How very small I must look, right up here. Anxious though he would be, I knew that the Captain would remain calm. And my little boy – how upset he would be that he hadn't seen me come back. I felt that I had let him down.

How cold it was becoming. I glanced at the aneroid. Over twelve thousand feet. Higher than I had ever been before. The chill airs of altitude were seeping through my clothes. And the silence! It seemed to deepen the higher I went.

The ache was coming into my arms – but I must hold on. I *must*! The words that Baldwin had spoken in court flashed through my mind: "It is as unthinkable for me to let go as it would be for any gentleman on the Bench to lose his senses," he had said. Quite so, Mr Baldwin... quite so.

I could hang on just as long as I could keep my senses. I had to stay alert. Singing would help.

"Pale hands I've loved, beside the Shalimar," I sang to the silence.

"Goodbye, Dolly, I must leave you," I bawled to the balloon at the top of my voice, wishing it jolly well *would* leave me.

"There is a happy land, far, far away," I sang to my father, for it was the hymn that he would sing whenever he had problems.

How small my voice must have sounded in that great emptiness. What an insignificant speck I was, alone in a vast ocean of air. Or was I alone? In the grandeur of space I felt that I was very close to God, and took comfort from it. How could anyone doubt His existence, I wondered? Certainly no one who had witnessed these heavenly splendours could do so. I hope that He would help me now, and give me strength, and somehow bring me back to His sweet earth. The heavens were fine, I thought, but I would rather be down *there*.

So, as the light faded, I fought the solitude and the silence and the ache in my arms with every hymn and ballad and song that I knew.

Then without warning the light was dimmed and the distant earth disappeared altogether as I was enveloped in a moist, cold shroud, swaddled in clammy cotton wool. Cloud! I had entered a bank of cloud. It was cold. It was frightening. I shuddered. I longed for light. I longed to *see...*

Then just as abruptly as I had entered the cloud, I emerged from it, into a new world – into another vast hall of silence and space, this one floored with a fleecy white carpet and with the great dome of purple skies for a roof. There was nothing to suggest that the earth existed at all. There was just cloud and space – and the balloon and me.

I looked up at the balloon again. It had long ceased to be my friend. It was some grotesque monster now, relentlessly carrying me higher and higher, like some mad abductor hauling me off to a distant and secret lair.

So cold now... so cold! My hands were numb. I took them one at a time from the bar and blew on them in a vain attempt to get them warm. I mustn't let them go to sleep. If they went to sleep, I would fall. One at a time I bit the ends of my fingers, to keep them awake.

I was hardly aware of the passage of time. It was measured by the changing colour of the sky, from vivid blue through a quick succession of yellows and reds as the sun left it. Then there was nothing below me. Nothing but blackness. The moon came to relieve the gathering darkness and the eerie solitude, but there was no longer light enough to see the face of my aneroid. I esti-mated that I was at fifteen thousand feet. Over two miles above the earth – if the earth was still there. I could hardly believe that it was. The stars popped out to look at me hanging there in their world, and seemed close enough for me to reach out and touch. Their twinkle gave hope to my dulling senses.

How much longer could I hold on? Was I still rising? Or coming down yet? There was no way of telling. How long would it be before my grip weakened, or my senses failed me?

"You'll do it once too often," so many of my friends had warned me. I began to talk to them, and to my family... talking out loud to them as I swung gently through the night, numb with cold and with the ache in my arms. "Once too often" they had said. Was this it? Was this the 'once too often'?

What would it be like, falling through the darkness when I let go? And when I hit the ground, would I *feel* it? Would I feel that fatal 'crump'?

Time by now had lost all meaning. Life itself seemed unreal. I was almost oblivious of the need to hold on to the thin strip of wood that separated life from death.

'If I should plant a tiny seed of love
In the garden of your heart...'

No, it wasn't me singing... strains of music were drifting gently through the night. I thought that my mind was slipping. It was time to go. Time to put an end to these hallucinations. Time to put an end to the cold and the pain.

'Would it grow to be a great big love some day
Only to die, and fade away...'

The tune persisted. I fought my way out of the dream world into which I was slipping and where I would have died. I tightened my grip on the bar. I took a new hold on life. I strained my ears into the blackness around me.

'Or would you care for it and tend it every day
Until the time that we must part...'

There was no mistaking it now! It was a band – a *real* band, not a heavenly one, – playing in the darkness somewhere below me. I was coming down... I was coming down!

With renewed strength I clung to the bar, trying to see through the obstinate cloak of darkness below me. The music had faded now and gone. I couldn't have dreamt it... could I?

Then without warning the blackness below me turned to grey, and suddenly I was lying on soft grass.

The bar slipped from my deadened fingers, the sling was dragged from between my legs, and with something like a quiet sigh, the balloon – relieved of my weight – disappeared back into the night like a huge bat, taking with it the empty, trailing parachute.

I lay there, exhausted, but for how long I didn't know. It was so peaceful, just to lie there. Suddenly there was a velvety touch on my cheek. I couldn't understand what it was. I didn't really care. I was too tired, too weak to be frightened by anything else that might happen to me. It came again, that soft touch, then a friendly snort. It was a horse. Then two or three of its friends came over to pay their respects to this strange visitor to their field.

I sat up. Strength gradually returned. I stood, shivering with the cold in my bones, and peered through the night for any signs of life. Away in the distance was a tiny glimmer of light. In the darkness I could find no gate, so I clambered with difficulty over the hedge and set off down the lane – and there, of course, was the gate just twenty feet further on! The walking gradually restored my circulation, but it was a long mile before I eventually reached the friendly glimmer that came from the window of a small cottage.

Wearily but thankfully I knocked on the door. An upstairs

window was thrown open and a white nightcap appeared! Almost simultaneously the front door opened, and a girl in night attire and holding a candle called back up the stairs, "Muther, there's a mon".

"No," I said, "I'm a girl, not a man."

Before I could say any more, the whole family was craning through the door and staring unbelievingly at the apparition before them. Never before had they set eyes on a female in a knickerbocker suit. Where had she come from? Who was she? What did she want at this time of night? I could read the questions in their faces.

"*Please* may I come in?" I pleaded. "I'm so cold and thirsty... and I don't know where I am."

Recovering from their surprise, they took me in without more ado. "You're in Whissendine," said Father as he lit an oil lantern. He then put a match to a big wood fire. While Mother prepared a hot drink, one girl fetched a blanket, and the other two little ones just stood there gawping. Oh, that mug of steaming cocoa – it was the best that I had ever tasted! As I sat there relishing every sip, wrapped in the blanket and thawing out before the blaze, I told them my story. The whole family listened, spellbound. They could only take my word that I had arrived by balloon, for I certainly had no balloon to prove it!

As I began to feel more like myself again, I realized how desperately anxious Captain Gaudron would be. I had to get a message to him, and the only way to do so at that time of night was through the railway station's telegraph system. I asked if there was a station nearby.

"Yes, there is," Father advised me, "but it is a mile and a half away and will be closed at this time of night – it's after midnight."

I couldn't face another walk. "How can I get there? Is there a pony and trap?" I asked.

There wasn't. But Father had a bicycle and offered to take me on it if I could stand on the back step. It appeared that my adventures for the night were not yet over.

The family were not going to miss this novel experience,

and dressed speedily as Father prepared his machine. So, in the darkness of the night and in the depths of the country, off we set along the unmade roads to the station – Father in the lead on his bicycle, me standing astride the rear wheel and holding on to his shoulders, Mother trotting along behind and the three children following in single file. After much puffing, blowing and wobbling, our strange procession reached the station, where we knocked up the bleary-eyed master. He stared as if in a dream at our incongruous assembly, and my story hardly convinced him that he *wasn't* dreaming. He quickly recovered from his surprise and agreed to send an urgent message.

With loud farewells the family set off on their return journey, leaving me in the hospitable hands of the station-master and his wife, by now also raised from sleep. The special communications system used by the railways was at last put into operation,and the station-master tapped out the message to Leicester in morse code, by moving the handle attached to the wall in his office backwards and forwards.

I knew how relieved Captain Gaudron would be to hear that I was safe, for it was over six hours since my dramatic disappearance. Arrangements were made for me to catch the six-thirty train in the morning, and in the meantime I was able to have a wash and a much-needed meal, then a few hours sleep before being roused for breakfast.

The station master's wife was most kind and understanding, but she was shocked at the thought of a young lady being seen in public wearing knickerbockers and insisted that I should wear one of her own skirts for my journey. I could hardly refuse. The trouble was that she stood five-foot-nothing to my five-foot-ten, so that when I wriggled into the light tan skirt over the top of my navy-blue knickerbockers, it barely reached my knees in front, and the train only just touched the bottom of my calves at the back. I must have looked very peculiar – but respectable!

When the train steamed into Leicester it was seven o'clock, Captain Gaudron was at the entrance to greet me and to escort me straight away to an open, horse-drawn carriage. The news of my arrival must have leaked out, because even at that early hour of the morning there were people on both sides of the street to cheer as I was driven away. I felt like royalty!

Relaxing in the hotel, I told Captain Gaudron what had happened. He could only think that the cotter pin had become jammed in some way in the release mechanism, to prevent me from pulling away. There had apparently been great consternation among the crowd, but he had assured them that I would keep calm and would eventually land safely. The pony and trap that he sent in pursuit had followed on the ground until my disappearance into cloud. We estimated that I had drifted about thirty-five miles into Rutland and had been clinging to the trapeze bar for well over three hours. I was very tired, and my arms ached terribly for several weeks, but otherwise I seemed none the worse for the ordeal.

We returned to London empty handed, with no need for porters to handle the balloon. It was found three days later, with the parachute still attached, floating in the North Sea. I was only glad that it had paused en route to put me down!

"Suddenly there was a velvety touch on my cheek..."

6

Chimney-pots and other strange places

Although potentially fatal when they did occur, aerial mishaps that arose from some malfunction of the balloon or parachute were rare events. Most of the injuries sustained by parachutists in those days came from landing in unlikely and quite unplanned places as the result of fickle and unpredictable winds.

Remember that we had very little control over our parachutes – unlike today with highly manoeuvrable canopies that can be 'flown' to a pin-point landing. The best we could do was to haul on the cords in an attempt to give some small impetus to the 'chute, on the principle that if you pulled down part of the canopy, the extra pressure in that direction would combine with the escape of air from the other side to give it a 'push'. With experience we became quite proficient at steering our parachutes in this way, but on the whole we were very much at the mercy of the winds. If we judged them wrongly, or if there was an unlucky shift in their direction or a change in their strength, there was nothing we could do about it.

I certainly landed in some strange places in my time...

Like poor Viola Kavanah I once had the misfortune to land on a roof-top, although with less tragic consequences. It was during a two-day event at Wolverhampton in 1910. The first day was calm and sunny, and everything went according to plan – what I used to call an uneventful 'up-and-downer'. On the second day, although it remained fine, the wind decided to wake up.

Despite the dubious conditions, there were large crowds at the showground hoping to see me make a descent from beneath the basket of a 'right-away' balloon and as I mingled with the people, I assured them that, unless the weather got much worse, I would not disappoint them.

"I have never cancelled a descent yet," I told them, "and I have no intention of doing so on account of a little wind."

Meanwhile, Captain Gaudron had been supervising the inflation of the balloon. It was just about ready to go when the wind suddenly decided to change direction. If I ascended from this position, I would undoubtedly be carried over the town, so it was decided to take off from the other side of the park in order that I might still be able to land within it before being blown into the rows of buildings beyond. Spectators had the novel experience of seeing the fully inflated balloon being guided across the park by a dozen or so men. It looked like some prehistoric, multi-legged monster toddling across the park on tiny feet!

Re-established in the arena that had been set aside for the athletes, and with its basket now attached, the balloon became aware that it was about to be reinstated to its former important function and that its mission was about to be fulfilled. Quivering with excitement, it tugged impatiently at the ropes that held it. In any wind at all, a tethered balloon can become a very wilful creature.

Whilst the Captain escorted his three passengers into the basket, I took up my position with what the newspapers chose to call my 'usual *sang froid*'.

"Hands... OFF!" came the command.

Once given its freedom, the balloon soared upwards with gay abandon, hauling me with it to the customary acclamation of the crowd. In the gusty, turbulent air, I was swung about more than usual beneath the basket during the ascent, but fortunately the canopy and cords remained untwisted, and I was able to pull away smoothly enough at the Captain's order.

The oscillation of the parachute as I descended was also more vigorous than usual. It certainly was gusty! Even so, it seemed that I would just about land in the open space that the Captain had obviously selected for me – or would I? Those buildings – they were getting awfully close! Then everything was happening so quickly...

That beastly wind seemed to take hold of me and sweep me towards the rows of roof tops, and I was powerless to stop it. A slope of dark grey slates was suddenly before me... chimney pots loomed up...

With a crash and a clatter and a very loud "Ouch!", I hit the roof.

Instinctively I let go of the trapeze bar and flung my arms round the only support that was offered. I had never thought I would embrace a chimney pot with such warmth. Looking round, I saw my 'chute gliding down into the garden below, taking several slates with it. If I had not let go, I would have been dragged from the roof with it, like Viola. But my troubles were not over. Clinging to my chimney pot with ever-growing affection, I wondered how on earth I was going to get down.

From my vantage point I had a perfect view of a long, narrow street that one moment was empty, and the next – as though by magic – was full of people. They seemed to come from everywhere, thronging from doors and side-streets until the road was one mass of upturned faces. Usually I enjoyed a good audience, but not on this occasion. They scared me stiff! While I was gazing down at them gazing up at me, the top of a ladder appeared above the guttering, followed by a reassuring face.

"Just let yourself slide down the roof," said the face, "and I'll catch you. You'll be all right."

"I'd rather drop from the clouds!" I told him.

"You'll be all right. Come on now – I'll catch you," he coaxed.

Despite his confidence, I was afraid that I would either knock him or the ladder over or miss him altogether, but I couldn't stay there, so taking a deep breath I let go of my chimney pot and slithered down the steep slates. Oh, those six feet were worse than a two-hundred foot drop from the balloon before the 'chute opened! But my rescuer was as good as his word. He caught me by the ankles, then helped me on to the ladder and down to safety, to a resounding cheer from the crowd, which the newspapers were later to number at two thousand. All to watch me climb down from a roof! I felt so silly...

The owner of the house had appeared by now, looking very puzzled by all the commotion. It appeared that he was a nightwatchman by trade and had experienced a very rude awakening from his daytime sleep.

I thanked my rescuer sincerely and learned that he was a Mr Herbert Spencer, a Great Western mechanic. I collected my parachute and threaded my way through the throng back to the park, none the worse for my escapade. As I appeared on the bandstand, I received the usual applause from the crowd, and the conductor turned to greet me, baton in hand. On impulse, I took it from him and proceeded to conduct the Band of the Coldstream Guards, which played on as though unaware of a change of leadership – to the great delight and amusement of everyone.

I was fortunate to have another 'Sir Galahad' close at hand when I landed in even more embarrassing circumstances during a show at Ashby, also in the Midlands. Again it was a windy day, with the added complication of a layer of low cloud. In order to keep within view, I had to pull away from my solo balloon before disappearing into this cloud. This, and the vagaries of the wind, made it difficult for me to select a landing-spot, but I had been carried over open countryside where there were plenty of green fields and no apparent hazards, so away I went. The canopy blossomed perfectly, but once again I was swung about more than usual by the turbulent air. When I was close to the ground, the wind took complete control, swung me round and hurled me backwards into a high barbed-wire fence.

There I hung, impaled on the spikes, my feet off the

ground, and both hands above my head still clutching the trapeze bar, whilst the parachute continued to billow and tug on the other side of the fence. I could feel the barbs digging into the back of my thighs, and I became aware that the lower part of my uniform had been ripped from my waist and was hanging down over my knees. I was quite unable to move – pinned there by the pull of the parachute in the wind, and unable to release it because on this occasion I *had* worn the 'safety belt'. What a predicament I was in! And painful, too. I was only glad that I had been swung backwards into the fence and not forwards, for there was a little more padding behind me. Even so, I was in great pain as the barbs tore into my flesh, and I was hoping desperately that help would arrive soon.

And so it did – in the form of a young gentleman who had been walking by himself in the fields when he had observed my arrival, and who now came hastening to my aid. What a sight I presented to him, strung up on the fence like a sacrifice, with the lower half of my knickerbocker suit hanging around my knees! The poor man turned as red as a beetroot and tried to avert his eyes from the unintentional display of underwear. But this was no time for modesty.

"Please!" I gasped, "Undo this belt around my waist. Hurry – please!"

Still trying to keep his eyes turned from my state of undress, his fingers fumbled at my waist and finally succeeded in releasing the clasp of the belt. I was able to let go of the bar and of the parachute, and instantly fell forward, almost into my rescuer's arms. Still blushing to the roots of his hair, he very carefully unhooked me from the spikes and helped me down to my feet. I was almost in a state of collapse. Taking off his coat, he gallantly held it in front of me as a screen behind which I could re-adjust my knickerbocker suit! It was torn and bloodstained, for the backs of my thighs were badly lacerated. I gladly accepted the large white handkerchief that I was offered, to wipe away the worst of the blood. By the time that the usual retinue of followers and the pony and trap had arrived on the scene, I was reasonably presentable, and my new-found friend had collected and rolled my parachute for me.

I was too embarrassed to tell anyone what had happened, and the manner of my landing and rescue remained a secret between Bert Wilton and myself, for we became good friends after that encounter. We would meet whenever I had a show in Ashby, and corresponded for many years.

An excess of wind and the nasty weather that accompanied it also caused me to land in an unlikely spot when I gave a show in Scotland. It was also the occasion of yet another unexpected encounter with a gentleman...

I have always remembered so vividly the clatter, clatter, clatter of clogs on the streets of Carlisle where we changed trains. At our destination we were met as usual by members of the Fête Committee. My word, what fine-looking men they were, and how I admired the swing of their kilts!

"You must be tired after your long journey," said one of our hosts to Captain Gaudron. "Will you and your bonnie lassie take a wee dram?"

The Captain accepted gladly, but his 'bonnie lassie' was aghast to find herself holding a tumbler that was three-quarters full of neat whisky! I could only sip it very gingerly, which caused the men to laugh heartily. The evening in their company proved a very happy occasion, and conversation over and after dinner was most animated.

The next morning was bright and sunny, and we set off early to prepare for the afternoon's events. As there was no supply of gas available it was necessary for us to use the hot-air balloon, so the Captain was soon fully occupied in supervising the digging of the fire-trench and the preparation of the balloon itself. As usual there were plenty of volunteers for these tasks.

I mingled with the crowds as they gathered, and found the people to be every bit as friendly as those of the Midlands and the southern counties where I usually appeared. I loved their soft accents, and those men in their kilts – oh, how proud and fine they looked, and so colourful in their various tartans! The hours passed quickly in such company, and it was soon time for me to change into my parachuting outfit, for the fire in the trench was going well, and the big black bag that hung between its poles above the 'chimney' was showing signs of life.

When I reappeared, I was disappointed to see that the sky was becoming overcast. All was ready for the ascent, however, the balloon was bulging with its load of hot air, and the parachute was connected and awaiting me. Even as I began to check the 'chute, the sun was obscured by dark, threatening clouds, and a few drops of rain fell as though as a warning. The crowd gave a loud and communal moan, and their mood changed instantly from joy to gloom beneath a suddenly leaden sky.

"Will there be an ascent?" everyone was asking. "Will she go?"

Members of the committee hastened to Captain Gaudron. "What is going to happen, Captain? Is it possible to have a show now that the weather has changed?"

Looking up at the ominous skies as though for inspiration, he replied in his usual calm manner. "Oh, I think we can manage it." Then he turned and looked inquiringly at me. "But the decision must be left to Miss Shepherd."

The decision was made without hesitation. "Of course I'll go," I said. "And the sooner the better, or the air inside the balloon will start to cool."

The news spread rapidly, and the people were delighted, although I noticed that many of them continued to look apprehensively at the rolls of cloud above, as though anxious for my safety. Yes, I thought – this could be a rough ride. It would be as well to leave my hat behind. I took it off and tied my long hair back in preparation for a tussle with the elements.

Even before I became airborne, I was in for a shock. I had taken my place astride the sling and was holding the bar, and was just about to give the order for the release of the balloon when without any warning a burly figure in a wildly swinging dark green kilt came rushing at me, snatched me from the trapeze and completely bowled me over. His charge was so forceful and I was so surprised that we both overbalanced and tumbled into the open part of the fire-trench, amongst the still smouldering embers. I don't mind telling you, we jumped out even more quickly than we had gone in! I recognized my assailant as one of the committee – a very tall and handsome man, whose fine physique and ginger-haired legs I had been secretly admiring earlier on. But even so – what on earth did he think he was doing, bowling me over like that? He hastened to explain that, just as I was about to set off, he had seen a spark inside the mouth of the balloon and had feared that the fabric would catch fire at the very moment that I was lifted from the ground. My indignation turned immediately to gratitude for this prompt and gallant action. Then, looking down at those fine legs, I noticed that he had not escaped entirely unscathed from the fire trench.

"Oh!" I blurted out, "All those lovely hairs have gone!" We both burst out laughing.

The spark had died within the balloon, which was still anxious to be off. The Captain also was anxious that we should be on our way before the air cooled and before the weather became any worse. I glanced upwards at the gathering clouds as I hurriedly took my position again. It didn't look at all promising, but I had never cancelled a show yet, and I didn't intend to start now.

"LET GO!" I cried.

A short run forward as the big bag of hot air rose at last from the ground, and I was hauled into the sky beneath it. Even as I was swept over the upturned faces of the crowd, I heard in the distance a low rumbling, as of drums, and the wind seemed suddenly to come with it, to swing me like a human pendulum beneath the balloon. I had been right – it was gong to be rough! The sooner I got down, the better – but I had to gain height before I could pull away in safety.

Suddenly, there was a vivid streak of lightning, so close that I felt I could have reached out and grabbed it. Then another, followed by a deafening clap of thunder, like a cannon going off in my ear. I was not normally afraid of storms, but to be up there in the middle of one – well, that was something new! It was a most eerie and frightening experience, and I gave an involuntary shudder at every flash and bang. I felt that I was in the middle of a battle, being shot at from all sides!

I had barely reached a thousand feet, and although it was much lower than my normal dropping height, the middle of an electric storm seemed to be no place to dally. I would have to take a chance and pull away now. Looking down hopefully for a safe landing spot, and seeing a nice green field with only a few buildings and trees beyond it, I wasted no further time and tugged the release cord. I prayed that at such a low altitude my 'chute would open immediately. To my great relief it did so, and I was soon heading out of the storm and back to earth, with the thunder still crackling over my head and the lightning seeming to chase me.

As I came down out of the storm, I soon realized that my troubles were not yet over, for the force of the wind was now such that I was being swung quite violently beneath the canopy and was also being blown over and beyond the field that I had selected as my landing-place. I was suddenly aware of wind-tossed trees beneath my feet... of a building looming close. Somehow I missed these obstacles and thumped awkwardly and rather heavily to earth, to finish up in a sitting position on a small mound, leaning against a slab of stone that I took at first to be part of a wall. Then I noticed that there were other little mounds and other slabs of stone all around me. It was on a grave that I was sitting and against a tombstone that I was leaning. I had landed in a cemetery!

When I tried to leap to my feet, I found that the force of my arrival in this unlikely spot had knocked the heels off both my boots. As I hobbled awkwardly amongst the headstones, rolling up my 'chute, I was overjoyed to hear the sound of a horse's hooves between the intermittent rumblings of the thunder, for this was a place where I had no wish to linger. Captain Gaudron's familiar face soon appeared, and he was as relieved to see me as I was to see him.

The rain started to pelt down as we made our way back to the fête grounds in an open cart, but despite the downpour the people surged out of the marquees to welcome me back. This sudden summer storm soon ended, the sun came out again and the fête continued.

"I don't want another trip like that!" I told the Captain when it was all over.

Fate had another unusual landing place prepared for me, however, when I undertook a show at Grantham. It was a town that greeted us with royal acclaim:

'Miss Dolly Shepherd the parachute Queen and Monsieur Auguste Gaudron the King of Balloonists,' declared the posters.

The usual extravagant claims were made for the double descent that we were to give, with fanciful illustrations of us clinging together beneath a single parachute, and talk of a 'race from the clouds'. We were indeed to give a double display, but not on one 'chute! We would ascend together, but each with our own 'chute attached to opposite sides of the balloon. We would also pull away quite separately. I was to go first, followed by the Captain, who would operate the ripping-cord. A double descent of this nature was merely another way of adding to the spectacle.

After the usual 'showing', I left the arena to change into my parachuting outfit, and when I returned to the enclosure, I was greeted by my father, who had travelled unexpectedly from London for the occasion. He always took a lively interest in my escapades and showed no fear for my safety – as this incident was to prove. He was the only member of the family ever to watch my 'madcap stunts'.

Our take-off was uneventful, and the Captain and I were soon sailing up into the blue, enjoying the splendid scene as it spread itself below, and chatting as we usually did across the eight feet or so that separated us as we perched in our slings and swung pleasantly beneath the majestic balloon.

"Doesn't that stretch of water sparkle with the sun on it?" I remarked. "What is it?"

"It is the Nottingham-Grantham canal," he said, "and that is the main railway line alongside it."

"What do you think of the posters showing the two of us descending on the one parachute?" I asked him.

"Nonsense," he chuckled. "That is a fantasy of the printers. It could never happened in reality." Neither of us knew that the day would come when it *would* happen in reality – to *me*!

"Now," said my airborne companion, looking at his aneroid. "You had better get ready to go."

"Oh no, not yet!" I protested. "Don't you remember what the posters said – a race from the clouds at a height of six thousand feet, and here we are at only three thousand."

"Never mind the people and the posters," he said sharply. "You look after yourself and pull away now."

Still playing for time so that we might go higher, I ignored his remarks. "My father is supposed to be following in the trap," I said. "I wonder if..."

"Will you *please* pull away now," he directed sternly. "We are over four thousand!"

From the tone of his voice I knew that four thousand was as far as we were going to go.

"Bye then – see you later," I called across the space that separated us, and pulled hard on my liberating cord.

The Captain followed almost immediately, but there was no question of a 'race' as we both floated gently down under our opened parachutes towards the distant earth. Indeed, we seemed to drift quite a long way apart at the whim of the breezes, and as I approached the field in which I hoped to arrive, I gave all my attention to the landing. I was altogether oblivious of my proximity to the canal and the railway line until the shining rails appeared directly below me. At the very same instant I heard a ferocious snorting and rumbling noise, and to my horror a train appeared as from nowhere, belching steam and charging straight towards the spot where I was about to land!

I barely had time to say to myself, more in disbelief than in fear, "I'm going under the train", and to tense myself in anticipation of the fatal impact, when the locomotive roared below me like a maddened beast. I was suddenly enveloped in an explosive blast of hot, smelly air, the force of which caught my parachute like a sail, so that instead of hitting the train, I was blown to one side. My feet skimmed the roof of a speeding carriage as I was swung violently under the canopy, and the next moment I was dumped quite unceremoniously on the ground alongside the track, with the noise of the train rattling away into the distance.

I lay there in a daze for a moment, quite bewildered by the unexpected encounter. I don't know to this day if that engine driver had seen me and, realizing that I was about to collide with the train, had purposely let off steam. If so, he showed great presence of mind and most certainly saved my life.

As I scrambled to my feet, I turned round and to my astonishment found myself looking rather foolishly at my own reflection – in the canal. I had landed on the narrow strip of land between railway and waterway. A few feet in either direction and I would have been very wet or very squashed!

The rolling up of the parachute was watched by a handful of people who came running to offer assistance, having seem me descend so near to the canal. They had fully expected to have to pull me out of it.

"That was a narrow escape!" panted one of them. "And an express train too! Are you hurt?"

"Oh no, I'm used to bumps," I said as nonchalantly as I could. I certainly wasn't used to dodging express trains and canals, though!

When the pony and trap arrived to collect me a few moments later, I was disappointed to see that Dad was not with it.

"Where is my father?" I asked the driver. "I thought he was following and was with you."

"Well... he wanted to... you know... so we left him at the Inn, just down the road," stuttered the poor man.

"Oh, I understand!" I said. "We'd better collect him on the way back."

Sure enough, when we reached the Boat Inn, there was Dad chatting happily with a local over a tankard of beer.

"Hello, Dolly," he said. "Why aren't you wet? We heard

you'd dropped into the canal?"

"I didn't drop *in* it – I just fell on the edge," I said. "And you're a fine one! I thought you were going to follow me and come and pick me up."

"Well, Dolly – I did follow most of the way. Then I heard you were safely down. I knew you'd be all right, so this gentleman and I are drinking your health."

Such was my father's confidence in me!

Canals and express trains; roof-tops and cemeteries; barbed wire fences – these were fortunately rare hazards. More likely obstacles were the numerous trees that always seemed to be standing around to watch us wherever we jumped in those days. Like little green bushes they looked from several thousand feet, clumped together in patches or lined like sentries along the edges of the fields for which we aimed. The clumps could usually be given a wide berth by carefully selecting our release point, but we had to keep a wary eye open for those sentinels that guarded the open spaces. They would grow taller as we descended, standing quite still, pegging their shadows to the ground, watching us. I came close to several of them, and I suppose I was quite lucky to make the acquaintance of no more than one tree during my parachuting career.

It happened in Monmouth, which until this descent in 1907 had been unknown territory to me. The only other occasion on which I had visited Wales had been on holiday, when I had climbed Snowdon and Cader Idris, reaching the summit of Arthur's Chair by way of the Foxes' Path. Being the only girl in a party of four young men, I had not dared to show my fatigue, nor the fact that my feet were raw with blisters. Back in the hotel, a kindly and sympathetic chambermaid had patched up my heels and toes with large quantities of adhesive plaster, to enable me to dance the night through. So, when I received the Captain's 'marching orders' for Monmouth, I wondered what Wales had in store for me this time.

On a warm Saturday afternoon in August, Captain Gaudron and I were met at May Hill station in Monmouth and taken to a fine hotel in Agincourt Square, where a reception had been arranged for the evening. Dinner passed pleasantly, conversation being centred on the history of the town, and the forthcoming Sports and Carnival on the Bank Holiday Monday.

That year the Mayor of Monmouth was the Honourable John MacLean Rolls, the eldest son of Lord and Lady Llangattock who lived at The Hendre, and the older brother of the well-known balloonists and motor car enthusiast Charles Rolls.

Charles Rolls had been one of the founders of the Royal Aero Club. In 1901, on a flight from the Crystal Palace in the balloon *City of York*, he had been accompanied by those other well-known aeronauts Percival Spencer and Mr Hedges Butler, with the latter's daughter Vera as passenger. Drifting high above London, they had discussed amongst other things the recent achievement of Santos Dumont in circling the Eiffel Tower in his small dirigible, a feat for which he had received a prize of £4,000 from the Aero Club of France. Why not, it was suggested, form a similar club in Great Britain? By the time that the *City of York* settled gently to the ground at Sidcup, the project had been thoroughly discussed, and the 'Aero Club of the United Kingdom' – later to become the 'Royal Aero Club' – was subsequently registered at Somerset House. Charles Rolls had furthered his reputation as an international balloonist by gaining third place in the prestigious Gordon Bennett balloon race in Paris in 1906, and he was now turning his attention to heavier-than-air flight as introduced to the world by the Wright Brothers only a few years before. At the same time his interest in motor cars had led him into partnership with Henry Royce, and together these two far-sighted pioneers had vowed to produce nothing but the highest quality in the automobile field. The citizens of Monmouth were justifiably proud of Charles Rolls and held high hopes for his future in the air and on the roads.

Sunday was always a quiet and uneventful day in Wales, with no newspapers and most people attending church or chapel. So, in order that I might be suitably entertained, I was introduced to a young man, Mr Edwards, the son of a former mayor. The committee considered that he would be a respectable, reliable and responsible escort, and it was arranged that he would show me the beauties of the countryside, and that we would visit Tintern Abbey for a raspberry tea. As I was able to ride, it was decided that we should go on horseback.

According to plan, my escort called at the hotel the following day with our two horses. The formalities over, he assisted me to mount. Sitting side-saddle and properly erect, I settled myself comfortably and adjusted my long skirt to ensure perfect decorum. Mr Edwards mounted his steed, and off we set at a walking pace across the cobble stones to the other side of Agincourt Square, where we paused at the railings for the commencement of my conducted tour.

"Over there, across the river," he said, pointing with outstretched arm, "is the Castle Field, which in 1233 was the scene of the Battle of Monmouth."

I observed demurely that it all looked very peaceful now, and listened with interest as my guide expounded the beauties and history of the area. He really was quite handsome.

As we headed south and began to wind our way at a steady trot through the deep, wooded valley of the Wye, our conversation gradually turned from matters historical.

"Do you do much riding, Miss Shepherd?" he asked. "You look so at home on a horse."

"Oh yes. I ride whenever I get the chance. When I was younger, I'd have to go out with a bridle to catch our horse from the common, and then ride him home bareback. I was quite a tomboy then."

"I can hardly believe *that* – you look so elegant now," he complimented me. "Shall we canter?"

With a nod of approval and a word to the horses, we were away, enjoying the invigorating air and drinking in the beauty of the countryside. Arriving at Tintern Abbey, we dismounted and my companion took the horses to tether them nearby. When he rejoined me, we settled to enjoy our raspberry tea and to admire the magnificent setting in which we found ourselves. It really was one of the most beautiful parts of the country that I had ever visited.

Our conversation inevitably turned to my involvement in parachuting, then to aeronautics in general. Mr Edwards of course was a keen supporter of Charles Rolls and shared the hopes of the people of Monmouth that he would be the first to fly in Britain. I reminded him that Cody was already ahead of Rolls with his man-carrying kites and was actually at that time building a powered machine that he was confident would fly. A friendly argument over the respective merits of these two great aerial pioneers ensued. One thing that we definitely agreed upon was that we ourselves were most fortunate to be living in an age when man seemed at last to be gaining mastery of the air.

By the time that our tea was finished, he was no longer Mr Edwards and I was no longer Miss Shepherd. We were Bunny and Dolly.

We spent an interesting half hour looking over the ruins of the fine old twelfth-century monastic buildings, then left the Abbey and strolled back to where the horses had been tethered. There was no sign of them.

We looked at each other in blank amazement for a moment, then burst into laughter.

"I suppose you *did* tie them up?" I asked, with perhaps a trace of suspicion in my voice.

"Oh Miss Shepherd – Dolly – how could you say such a thing!" he protested laughingly.

"Well, no one will *ever* believe us!" I chuckled. "Come on, we'd better go and look for them."

We set off through the woodland in search of the errant animals and eventually found them grazing peacefully about a mile away. We checked them, walked them back through the trees and mounted. Dusk was falling by now, but the air was mellow and still, and we filled the darkening valley with happy singing as we rode at a leisurely pace back towards Monmouth.

By the time that we reached the town, it was draped in its Welsh Sunday evening. All was dark and silent – until, like a squadron of cavalry, we came clipperty clopping into Agincourt Square! As the echoes of hooves on cobbles shattered the peace, one window opened, then another – then another. Heads appeared. Curtains were pulled aside. Curious eyes peeped. We chuckled quietly as we dismounted at the hotel, and as he bade me goodnight, poor Bunny whispered, "I shall never live this down!"

I slept well that night, to be awakened next morning by a knock on the door. "Come in," I called drowsily.

It was my breakfast, which I always had in bed on these occasions! Usually it was delivered by a chambermaid, but this time it was brought to my bedside table by a senior male member of the hotel staff. How honoured I was, I thought... then soon realized that there was nothing honourable about the visit at all, as the fellow tried to inflict his amorous intentions upon me.

These being unwelcome, I curtly dismissed him.

I immediately dressed and packed my bags. As I was signing out at the reception desk, I was implored not to leave, but such was my indignation that I would not stay there a moment longer. I walked across to the nearby Monnow Restaurant and asked the proprietor if he could accommodate me there for the rest of my stay in Monmouth. He was delighted and made me most welcome. In fact, when I left the next day, he told me that he was going to rename the restaurant after me, and 'The Dorothy' it was to remain until the early 1920s, when it became a grocer's shop.

It was time for the serious business of the day, and I soon put that little unpleasantness in the hotel from my mind. The day had begun misty, but the sun soon made its presence felt and by mid-morning was shining brilliantly from a cloudless sky. It was perfect Bank Holiday weather, and the crowds flocked early to the show, so that the meadow on the Old Dixton Road was soon alive with activity.

As usual, Captain Gaudron was busy supervising the inflation of my solo balloon, and I began my duties of 'showing myself'. As I mingled and chatted with the people, I was able to watch some of the events – the many foot races and athletic contests; the wrestling and tug-of-war – both on horseback; the gymnastic displays; the dancing; and the enchanting performance of the Band of the Royal Monmouthshire Royal Engineers. It was a most happy occasion. The air was alive with the spirit of the carnival.

As the time for my 'curtain call' came near, I went to change into my aeronautical outfit, then returned to the balloon enclosure. A gentle breeze had joined us, and after discussing the air conditions with the Captain, I meticulously checked every fold and cord of my 'chute before it was attached to the balloon. All was ready. The spectators hushed in anticipation as they watched me take up my position. At a nod from the Captain I gave the order to release the balloon. Immediately and gracefully it rose from the ground, and I was swept into the air beneath it, waving my silken Union Jack to the cheering throng. I knew that Bunny would be down there amongst those faces, perhaps a little anxious for my safety as he watched my diminishing figure dangling in space.

It was an absolutely breathtaking view that spread itself below me as I was lifted skywards. There were the two rivers that embraced the town – the Wye and the Monnow, their waters winking up at me in the sunlight, and the fine old fortified bridge striding boldly across the latter. As I rose higher, I could see the wooded slopes of the valley where Bunny and I had ridden so happily the day before, and I could just make out the grey walls of the Abbey in the distance. Oh, I was in my element, and thought how lucky I was to be swinging there in the silent sky, with such beauty laid out below as though for my very approval.

The time under the balloon was too short, as always. I was nearing four thousand feet. Time to pull away and return to that beautiful earth. There was a green patch just beyond the bend in the river. This breeze should carry me there quite nicely.

"Here we go!" I said to the parachute and, with a pull on the ripping-cord, fell into space. The welcome sound and the familiar tug of the opening parachute assured me that all was well, and an upward glance at the big silken umbrella confirmed it. For a while I continued to enjoy the scenic splendour as I floated lazily down, then I turned my attention to the serious business of landing.

Passing over the shining curve of the river, I seemed to be well on course for one of two fields on the far side – or was I? The wind appeared to hesitate, then began to sweep me slowly back across the water. Well, that was all right, for there were open fields on that side too. But that fickle breeze hadn't finished its little games yet. It seemed to be wandering about in the valley as though quite unsure which way to go, and now it changed its mind yet again, so that once more I was being carried across the river. The gently flowing waters of the Wye were now ominously close, and I realized with dismay that I was not going to reach the sanctuary of those fields after all. Even if I crossed the river, I could not hope to clear those tall trees that bordered it. I was going to get either wet or scratched! I wasn't sure which would be the more unpleasant, but in any case there was nothing I could do about it – the wind would decide.

As though tiring of the game at last, it eventually made up its mind and flung me with what I thought was quite unnecessary force into the very top of a tall oak. With a great crackling and snapping of twigs, I seemed to be plunging right through the foliage and instinctively flung out one hand to grab a branch, sill holding desperately to the trapeze bar with the other. Momentarily I hung there. Then came a sharp crack as the branch gave way, and my hand shot back to the trusty trapeze bar as I tensed myself for the drop. But I didn't fall. By now the canopy of my parachute had draped itself lovingly over the upper branches of the tree, and I was held fast, dangling in mid-air. I looked down to see where I was, and found that I was peering straight into the river as it flowed quite unconcerned some distance below. It could be, I thought, that I was going to get both scratched and wet. How unfair...

Help was at hand, however. Within minutes I heard voices and could see three pairs of eyes peering up at me from the bank, through the thick foliage.

"Hang on – we're getting help," called a familiar voice. I might have guessed that Bunny would be on hand to organize my rescue. There was discussion and commotion on the bank for a few minutes before another voice shouted,

"Can you hear me, up there?"

"Yes."

"I'm going to secure a rope to the next tree. When I throw it to you, catch it and swing over. Then you can slide down."

So saying, my rescuer climbed up the neighbouring tree, secured the rope and, having descended, threw it across to me. I transferred my trust to it from the trapeze bar, wriggled out of the sling and, feeling more ape-like than lady-like, swung from one tree to the other. From there I slid easily to the ground. There were thanks and congratulations all round.

What about that?" asked my rescuer, pointing up to the top of the tree, which wore my parachute like a dust-cap on the side of its head.

"We might damage it if we try to get it down," I said. "We'd

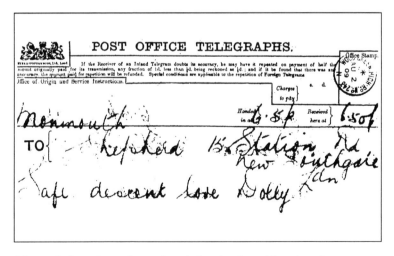

After each descent – and sometimes before it – I would send a telegram to my parents to let them know I was all right. This was sent from Monmouth, where on a previous occasion I had landed in a tree on the bank of the River Wye. The telegram cost sixpence, and was delivered in less than an hour.

better leave it just now, and Captain Gaudron will see about recovering it later."

Two men then came forward and gallantly offered to escort me back to the showground. One was a pleasant, distinguished-looking gentleman in his middle years, and the other was Bunny. The choice was obvious.

As we made our way to the pony and trap, and once out of earshot of the others, Bunny said, "Did you know who *that* was when you accepted my offer?"

"No. Who?"

"None other than the Bishop of Hereford!"

"Oh, I hope I didn't offend him!" I chuckled. "Anyway, I would much rather come with you."

Happier Landings

What happened to Bunny Edwards, you ask. A budding romance? No, not really. Bunny was one of many good friends I had made during those parachuting years – one of many companions who added much to the pleasure of being a lady parachutist of the Edwardian age, for those pleasures were not confined to the air.

For me, parachuting itself would have been sufficient reward. The sheer thrill of it more than compensated for the dangers that we courted. The serious mishaps that I have recounted were rare, and a few bumps and bruises were all part of the job. I never kept a record of the number of ascents and descents that I made, but it was well over a hundred and most of them were free of incident. Most of my landings were happy ones.

Yet although the exquisite pleasure of being lifted high into the air, then dropped gently out of it, was reward enough, there were other benefits associated with the life of a parachutist that made it almost as enjoyable on the ground as it was in the air. There was the adulation of the crowds; there was the entertainment that was accorded me wherever I appeared for a show; there were experiences and opportunities that came rarely to young ladies in those days; and above all there were the friendships that I made with people from all walks of life.

Wherever we went for a show, we were treated as VIPs. The best hotels, fine meals, excellent entertainment, the attendance of numerous gentlemen, and the applause of the crowds – all this and parachuting too! Can you wonder that I enjoyed those days?

Because the committees that organized the various fêtes and events at which we appeared were predominantly and often entirely male, we lady aeronauts were perhaps treated even more royally than our male colleagues, and our slightest whims were often pandered to. For instance, one August Bank Holiday stands out in my memory as an occasion on which I realized two of my youthful ambitions – and which began with an amusing encounter.

I was on my way to Ashby-de-la-Zouch in Leicestershire, travelling second class as usual. It was more comfortable than third, where some carriages still had sawdust on the floors, for spitting was not yet forbidden. When the time came for lunch, I made my way to the restaurant car and took a window seat. Before long I was joined by an attractive young man. It was not done for ladies to talk to strangers, but the passing of the condiments provided him with an opportunity to open the conversation, which then continued over a wide range of subjects. When he became so bold as to ask me my name, I evaded the question, but nothing daunted he continued the attack by complimenting me on my smart navy-blue dress. Contemplating my arms through the lace sleeves, he said, "You look as though you have strong arms."

With a flash of inspiration I said, "That's strange! That's my name – Armstrong." (It was a *nom de plume* that I was to use several times afterwards!)

Sensing that he was making progress, my companion then asked where I was going. I told him that I was travelling to Ashby-de-la-Zouch.

"Ashby!" he said, with obvious delight. "So am I – I'm going to see Miss Shepherd make a parachute descent. I know her quite well."

"You do?" I said.

"Oh yes," came the emphatic reply. "I've taken her out to dinner on several occasions."

"Really! How interesting."

I would have liked to have heard more about Miss Shepherd and his relationship with her, but I steered the conversation to other matters! When the train screeched to a halt at our destination, the young man opened the door for me, alighted and handed me out. Two members of the Fête Committee came towards me, with cheerful greetings.

"Hello, Miss Shepherd! I hope you've had a pleasant journey!"

"Yes, indeed I have," I replied, and looked round for the young man. He was already melting sheepishly into the crowd!

I was a frequent visitor to Ashby, where I always stayed at the Royal Bath Hotel. I was quite well known to the local populace, and the next day I was warmly welcomed by many friends when I mingled with the people in the Bath Grounds, where the fête was being held.

My performance took place in the late afternoon. It was, as expected, a happy 'up-and-downer', fully successful and without incident. It was *after* the parachute descent that one of my dreams came true, for instead of the customary pony and trap, what should arrive to pick me up from the field in which I had landed but a *motor car*! It was a great shiny beast, with much lovingly polished brass, and was the proud possession of Mr Shields, one of the committee members. It had long been one of my dearest wishes to ride in an automobile, for it was still considered a rare adventure. The fact that the machine spluttered and wheezed a great deal, that it went no faster than the pony and trap would have done, and that it stopped at frequent intervals and had to be pushed, did not detract from the thrill of the experience as I was carried back to the Bath Grounds in great style. I was particularly intrigued to watch the 'winding-up' of the vehicle by means of the starting handle. As usual, I wanted to be allowed to try it myself, but when I was warned of the danger of breaking a thumb or wrist by the kick of the handle, I declined. My hands were too valuable.

My second dream came true on the following day. I also had a great desire – probably more common amongst boys – to drive a train. When I happened to mention this during the course of conversation with members of the committee at Ashby, arrangements were made for their VIP to achieve her ambition. A railway inspector accompanied me to the station at Moira and on to the footplate of a locomotive, where I was introduced to the driver and fireman as co-driver for a short spell. The stoking was completed, the guard blew his whistle and waved his green flag, and the train puffed its way laboriously out of the station. As we rattled along, the driver explained the workings of a steam engine and then allowed mc to take control for a short stretch of the line. To my great delight he asked me at one point to pull the thin metal rod to set off the high pitched whistle that gave warning of our approach. Whenever I heard a train whistle after that, I used to think back to that happy day on the footplate. Alas, they don't whistle any more!

I was given an opportunity to drive a more traditional form of transport during one of several visits that I made to Pickering, where I had made that first solo ascent under a hot-air balloon.

It was the occasion of the Annual Gala, at which I was to make two parachute descents on the one day – one in the afternoon, the other in the evening. The first caused me some discomfort. I was again using the hot-air balloon, but this time it behaved itself rather badly. When it was liberated, it swayed ominously towards a large tree. It just managed to clear it, but I didn't! Swinging below it at the end of my parachute, I was dragged bodily through the upper branches, to my own and everyone else's consternation. I clung grimly to the trapeze bar as the thick foliage and twigs tried to drag me from it. One persistent branch tried to take hold of the parachute itself by becoming entangled in the cords, and I was forced to reach out and break it off. Then I was hauled up and out of the leafy labyrinth into clear air, where I waved vigorously to the people below to assure them that all was well. Despite the uninvited passenger still entwined in the parachute lines, the canopy opened normally when I pulled away from the balloon, and the descent was perfect. The evening performance was more straightforward and less painful, and I made a spectacular descent in a field opposite the Gala Grounds, thus giving everyone the unusual thrill of seeing me actually land as well as take off.

The following day, as part of my 'entertainment', I was invited to join a party for a delightful tour of the countryside in a four-in-hand wagonette. I was seated high up in front, next to the driver, where I was in my element. We left from the centre of this picturesque market town, passed the parish church of St Peter and St Paul and set off at a gentle trot through the wooded dale, with the crystal-clear stream wandering through it and the heather-covered moors above. The day was ideal for viewing such spectacular scenery.

Chatting to the driver, I told him that I had been used to horses all my life and asked if I might be allowed to take the reins. I could not resist the challenge of the open road that stretched before us! He was hesitant and somewhat apprehensive, but I finally persuaded him, and when he saw the competent way in which I handled the 'ribbons', his fears were allayed. I was soon singing happily to the rhythm of the hooves, and before long I had the whole party joining me in the refrain of 'On Ilkley Moor Baht' At'.

Class distinctions in Edwardian society were far wider and more clearly defined than they are today, and few people associated with those outside their own particular 'class'. I was therefore especially lucky to have opportunities to meet and make friends with people from all levels of society, and from all parts of the country.

Only the very poor – and there were unfortunately many of them – were not represented at the shows and fêtes where I performed. Quite simply, they could not afford the entry fee, modest though it was. The gaiety and apparent opulence of Edwardian life was not for all.

On the other hand, the 'working classes' provided a large proportion of my audiences, particularly in the Midlands, where the Wakes had become an important and popular feature in the newly emerged industrial societies. Wakes have their origins in religious celebration – the patronal festival of the local church. This developed in the late nineteenth century into a week's popular holiday, for the pleasure and amusement of the whole parish. Dates varied according to the feast-day of the saint to whom the church was dedicated. So it was that every village and town celebrated in its own way for a whole week, usually culminating in a grand fête in its local park, often lasting for two or three days.

Entrance to the fête would usually cost a shilling up to five o'clock, and sixpence after that. There would be a printed programme for a penny, about half of it devoted to advertisements, and the rest giving details of the 'Timetable of Events and Amusements'. There would be some thirty to forty events on the programme, commencing after lunch and continuing right through to the late hours of the evening. There would be athletic events, military bands, wrestling, conjurors, strongman acts, dancing competitions, theatrical performances, tumblers and jugglers, performing animals, pony races and bicycle races – plus all the attendant stalls and amusements. The final item was invariably a Grand Firework Display. And 'grand' they were, comprising a dozen major set pieces and up to fifty 'miscellaneous fireworks' – all specialized displays prepared and artistically staged by professional pyrotechnists, such as W & J Wilders of Birmingham. No fête would have been complete without this stupendous finale.

The major event of the day's entertainment, however, was undoubtedly the Balloon Ascent and Parachute Descent. This form of aerial exhibition had been thrilling the crowds during their Wakes and at other holidays since the early 1890s, when Baldwin had first demonstrated the limp parachute in Britain. One of those who followed after him had been Captain Gaudron, who had been appearing at the Midland Wakes since the latter part of that decade, so that by the time I joined his team, it was well known in the area. It was not unusual for us to have a two-day tour in connection with the Wakes, sometimes with two descents each day.

The fêtes were always a family occasion, with a great air

of jollity and innocent fun prevailing. The effect that my shows – and my knickerbocker suit – had on the local populace on such occasions can be illustrated by this report in a local paper on that particular show at Ashby when I rode in a motor car. It was written in the Derbyshire dialect by someone signing himself 'Roadster'.

"...*Wa soon finished up the 'snap' wa brawt wi'us, an thin wint te sae Dolly goo up in thi bloon. It 'ad a lot o'bags o' sand 'anging on wen wa got thear to ode it down. I arsked ma Emily Susan if shae cud sae Dolly, but shae cuddna, thin I copt eyes on 'er an' turned away – ma face did goo red. Emily Susan sed ti mae, "Willie Arthur, whativers thi matter wi yer? Yo luk loike a ode lobster." Thin shae had a luk round ti sae wat it wor that 'ad made ma goo so red, an' wen 'er eyes cort soight of Dolly in 'er bloon suit, well yo shud sae 'ow quick shae put 'er 'brella up.*

"*I 'ad another look thin, an' shae wor just getting reddy to goo up, an fellows war odin' bloon daown until a man shouted "lit go", an' away Dolly wint odin' on to thi 'shute an' weevin 'er 'and at us as 'ard as shae cud. Shae wint 'igher, 'igher, 'igher, till wa cud 'ardly sae 'er at all; thin shae samed ti snatch at thi 'shute an cam down a long way before it ud open, thin whin it did open shae cum down luvely, an' abart 'alf an hour arter, shae cum racin' in thi Bath Grounds agin in Mr Shield's motor car. Shae is a plucky gel, an' 'er wor loffing awey loike anything, an' paple wor cheerin' an' shoutin' as 'ard as war cud te let 'er no 'ow wa loiked 'er. Shae is a foine bonny lass wen yo cum close up to 'er, an' shae luked so noice an' jolly...*"

Many of the working lads whom I met at the shows – butcher boys, grocery boys, apprentices, sons of miners and factory workers – showed a lively interest in aeronautics and listened to me with envy when I spoke of the thrills of the air. Many of them were to achieve their own aerial ambitions in the Royal Flying Corps during the years ahead. Sadly, so many of them would be flying to their deaths. Some I actually met again during those war years. For instance, on one occasion when I was serving on the Western Front, I was driving a

General to a unit of the Royal Flying Corps. As usual, on arrival I jumped out and opened his door. The Guard of Honour was already formed up and about to salute. The Camp Commandant stepped forward. Obviously taken aback at seeing me, and momentarily forgetting the General, he rushed up to me and said, "Oh, it's Dolly Shepherd!"

In addition to entertainments arranged for me by member of the committee, I always received hosts of invitations to 'come for tea' from the people with whom I mingled before the shows. They were always so friendly and hospitable, and so proud of their homes and of their work. I remember in particular an occasion at Longton in the Midlands, when I really did see the working classes at work...

It was the annual two-day fête in June, and it was planned for me to make double descents there, with other girls of the Gaudron team, on two different days. On the Monday morning, while the Captain went to Queen's Park early to make the necessary preparations. I was escorted round the town by members of the committee and introduced to a number of prominent people. For these VIP appearances I was always smartly dressed. On this day I was wearing a pale grey suit, with long skirt and short train, a tight-fitting jacket trimmed with white, a white wide-brimmed hat and white gloves. As the morning wore on, imagine my horror when I realized that my complete outfit had changed colour – it was almost black!

My escort was most apologetic. "Someone should have warned you," he said. "This is a pottery town, and particles of soot and chemicals mix in the air and affect everything. Even our curtains don't last long – they rot and can't be washed."

"Fortunately I've brought another outfit – a darker one!" I laughed. "I shall have to go back to the hotel to change."

When I walked amongst the crowd that afternoon, I did in fact notice that the clothes they wore *were* darker than those of people in other parts of the country, but nonetheless smart. The ladies all wore long dresses, the little girls had frocks down to their calves, with black stockings and boots, and without exception men, women and children wore hats or caps. Such pride those people took in their appearance.

Viola Kavanah was to be my partner for that afternoon's descent from a right-away balloon – for this was of course before her tragic and fatal fall. She joined me, and as we strolled and chatted with the spectators, we were able to catch glimpses of the Punch and Judy show, the football match being played on bicycles, and the clowns. We also enjoyed the delightful music played by the Royal Marine Band from Chatham, especially the selection from *Pagliacci*.

The hours passed quickly and it was soon time for us to change into our parachuting costumes. Back we came, to be acclaimed by the friends we had made earlier in the day. When we had checked and prepared our 'chutes, they were attached to the netting on either side of the big silver balloon that stood so patiently in the still evening air. Everything was ready. The last passenger was climbing aboard, and the Captain was giving his final instructions. Viola and I perched ourselves on opposite sides of the basket, with legs dangling over the edge.

The Captain's "Hands… OFF" rang out loudly in the silence that had descended upon the spectators, and we rose gracefully into the blue, cloudless sky.

I had always enjoyed these leaps from the basket, partly because of the thrilling sensation of actually launching oneself into space, but also because of the company that one had during the ascent. The reactions of the passengers, most of them venturing into the air for the first time in their lives, were a source of interest and often of amusement. There were always those who would adopt an air of nonchalance and would talk loudly and laugh much whilst the basket remained anchored to the ground, but their bravado would evaporate with altitude, and there would be a certain whiteness about the knuckles as they gripped the wickerwork. Mostly their fears would be more than compensated for – if not completely overcome – by the sheer exhilaration of silent flight, and the awe-inspiring views from on high. Certainly, on such a quiet and splendid evening as this, there was no cause for our passengers to be concerned as we rose so peacefully and effortlessly into the clean air high above the sooty town.

"I could never have imagined such a wonderful feeling!" breathed one, in awe.

"What a fantastic view!" exclaimed another. "But how wide the pottery chimneys look!"

"Yes," I chirped happily from my perch. "That's the one thing I'm scared of – coming down into one of those. I don't think I'd made a very good Father Christmas!"

"Now, girls," said the Captain brusquely, "We're over two thousand feet – get ready to jump."

As they realized that the moment of our departure was approaching, our passengers lost some of their composure, and their smiles disappeared. They had the air of reluctant witnesses at an execution.

"You go first, Viola," I called.

The basket swayed gently. Viola was gone.

"You wouldn't get me doing that," gulped one of the passengers, peeping sheepishly over the edge and down on to the distant parachute that was now floating back to earth like an outsize dandelion seed.

"It's a glorious feeling," I laughed. "I'm off..."

So saying I sprang forward into space, leaving the three gentlemen peering apprehensively over the side of the basket.

"They don't know what they're missing," I mused as I revelled in the gentle descent beneath the fully opened, friendly canopy and eyed a soft-looking landing ground.

Within half an hour Viola and I were back at the show-ground, waving joyfully to the crowds from the bandstand. We then stayed on through the evening to watch the finale – the Grand Firework Display. It was our turn to look in wonderment. I never ceased to marvel at the ingenuity and variety of those fantastic set pieces. There was even a firework elephant that moved its trunk and tail, and the climax to over an hour's entertainment was a beautiful bouquet of flowers that changed to an enormous fire-picture of King Edward VII and Queen Alexandra.

The next morning Viola left for another engagement while

the Captain and I went to the fête grounds to carry out running repairs on the balloon, which had been slightly torn on landing the day before. We always had a repair kit with us, consisting of a small hand-operated sewing machine and pieces of balloon fabric. The Captain examined the balloon thoroughly, and when the tear was located, he held the edges taut while I machined a strip of fabric down it, then finished the last few inches by hand. The repairs completed, all was then made ready for another double descent that evening.

Flo Lusby joined me for this second show. The ascent and our descents were quite straightforward, apart from one small incident reported thus in the *Staffordshire Sentinel*: *'...Miss Shepherd's parachute struck a telephone wire, but this caused no inconvenience to the lady.'*

As always when 'showing ourselves' before a performance, Flo and I had received many invitations to visit people in their homes. When we returned to the bandstand after our drop, we were asked by the chairman of the committee if we would like to look over the potteries and also accept an invitation to have tea with a miner and his family. Flo had to return home, but I was most happy to accept.

What an interesting day it proved to be! In the morning there was a visit to the Dresden Pottery works to see the fascinating process whereby the clay was transformed from its natural state into articles of beauty renowned throughout the world. In one section men were working in the firing-ovens in such intense heat that periodically they collapsed and had to be taken to lie down on mattresses laid out in the fresh air of a 'recovery room'. As they revived, they returned to take their places again at the ovens. I then visited the 'inspection room', which was quite heart-breaking! Here, every piece of china was thoroughly examined, and if the minutest flaw was discovered, it was smashed.

During the afternoon I visited the homes of several miners, whose wives each persuaded me to 'put my feet under the table', so that by the time I reached the cottage of the foreman – Mr Barton – I was awash with tea!

Despite the constant intrusion of coal-dust and the smutty atmosphere outside, each home was spotlessly clean and possessed a piano which the children were learning to play. Notwithstanding their problems and occasional tragedies, they were a closely knit and happy community.

I was interested to watch Mrs Barton prepare her husband's bath in the small washroom at the back of the house. A big tin bath standing on the stone floor was filled with hot water from a copper by means of a special tin scoop with a wooden handle. I was ushered out, of course, before the actual ceremony. When a well-scrubbed Mr Barton joined us for tea, he announced that he had arranged for me to go down the pit and that his wife and two of her friends might accompany us. It would be an exciting experience for us all, as none of the other ladies had ever been down before.

I thought that I had got used to dropping long distances, but going down into the depths of the earth in that cage was a most unusual feeling. The cage was like a big box, with thick wooden sides black with coal-dust and dirt, and mounted on a steel frame. A 'banksman' dropped the gate, and down we went into utter blackness. There was no sensation of speed, but my legs felt as though they were loose, and my feet did not appear to be touching the floor. I felt as though I was suspended in a thick, black vacuum. Most eerie! As we dropped with a great rattling and clanking, the air became very cold at first, then warmer as the peculiar smell of coal-dust rose to meet us, until at last the cage shuddered to a standstill. There was a glimmer of light from the lamp of the 'gateman' as he raised the door, and there we were in a different world – the working world of the miner, so different from the vast open spaces to which I was accustomed.

As our eyes adjusted to the dim light, we followed Mr Barton along a main 'roadway' until the chip-chip of picks and the voices of men indicated our imminent approach to the coal-face. There were the colliers, stripped to the waist and covered with coal-dust, so that their eyes, caught by our lights as we approached, shone out like diamonds in the darkness. Despite the conditions in which they worked, they were a happy and lively group of men, linked together by the wonderful bond of camaraderie so often felt in the face of danger.

A strange noise caused us to turn suddenly. It was a pony, knocking a heavy curtain – known as a 'brattice' – aside with its head cap as it hauled its three wagons up to the face for filling. I was intrigued to learn how the ponies knew just what to do, where to go, where they had to stop to pick up the full wagons and where to stop again to have them emptied.

"They're almost human," Mr Barton said, "and they work a ten to twelve hour shift, the same as the men."

The animals were stabled underground and only came up into the light and the fresh air once a year, during the Wakes.

"I've seen them come up," said Mrs Barton. "They have to be led as they're almost blind at first, and then it's lovely to see them frolicking and scampering around the fields."

We continued our underground journey until Mr Barton stopped and pointed to a black figure lying on his side in a crevice. We stood and watched while the man hacked at the coal only a few inches above his head.

"Bill, you've got a visitor," called the foreman. As the man turned, one of our lady companions gave a cry of dismay:

"Oh no! It's my Bill! I won't ever grumble at him again when he says his arms ache."

I was curious to know what it felt like to work in such cramped conditions and was invited to find out for myself. So I changed places with the collier and, under instructions, took the pick and hacked away. When I rejoined the group, I had several pieces of coal, and a very black face!

As we were making our way back to the shaft, Mr Barton stopped abruptly and shouted to us to step back and stand still. Within a few yards of us there was a crackling noise in the darkness, followed by a rumbling. We stood motionless, startled out of our wits by a fall of coal, but our guide dismissed such happenings as 'all part of the day's work' and explained how an experienced collier like himself could feel the coming of a fall through his feet.

Despite his assurance, we were glad to reach the bottom of the shaft and climb into the cage! Unlike the strange lightness experienced during the descent, our feet felt like lead weights on the upward journey.

How wonderful it was to see the sun and the blue sky and to take deep breaths of fresh air! I thought of the ponies, who only came up once a year...

I thanked Mr Barton for the exciting experience. "Now that I have dropped from the heavens to the earth, and from earth into the bottomless pit, I think I will carry on with my parachuting," I said.

"And I'll stick to my pits," was the laughing reply.

Those pieces of coal that I hewed from the Florence Mine in Longton are still amongst my most prized possessions.

The more lasting friendships that I made during those years tended to be amongst the 'middle classes'. The members of the committees who organized the fêtes and shows were usually professional or sporting men, or persons of some local consequence, often including the mayor. They were always most friendly, and in their company I spent many pleasant evenings and enjoyed many an outing. Of course, there were people from all classes amongst the spectators, and several firm friendship developed from brief encounters whilst I was 'showing myself' before an ascent. On my first visit to Wolverhampton, for example, I had met a well-known and much-respected doctor and his wife. From then on, whenever I gave a display in the area, I stayed with them at Heathtown, and we became good friends.

Dr O'Brian was a middle-aged man, tall and slim. His tremendous sense of humour, his skill and his kindness inspired instant confidence, with the result that his practice was bursting at the seams. His surgery was always packed, with queues reaching out along the street. Mrs O'Brian was also a kind and sympathetic person, and a most useful assistant to her husband, for she had been a hospital sister. She was a very attractive woman, with burnished golden hair.

THRILLING ADVENTURE OF TWO LADY PARACHUTISTS.

B1: The artist of *The Illustrated Police Budget*, so typical of the period, shows a very vivid imagination but little attention to fact in this portrayal of the first mid-air rescue. Our costumes were not quite so daring!

HEROINES OF THRILLING PARACHUTE ADVENTURE.

GIRL'S FEARFUL
LEAP FOR LIFE.

From One Parachute to Another
Nearly Three Miles High.

COMPANION'S SACRIFICE.

Gallant Girl Injured in Attempt to
Save Her Friend.

One of the most thrilling stories ever related of escape from death is that connected with the balloon ascent and parachute descent of Miss Dolly Shepard and Miss Louie May, who went up from Longton, in Staffordshire.

It was originally intended, writes a "Lloyd's News" representative, that they should ascend in a large balloon, in which they would have had the company and assistance of Captain Gaudron, an experienced aeronaut, but it was found at the last minute that the valve would not be safe. A smaller balloon was, therefore, requisitioned, and the ascent commenced under favourable conditions.

At about 4,000 feet from the ground the two young ladies were to have released their parachutes, and in the ordinary course the balloon would then gradually collapse and descend.

Miss Shepard found her apparatus in excellent working order, but Miss May was at once in difficulties, entangled in the network, and unable to release her parachute. They were still ascending rapidly, and Miss Shepard might easily have made her ... ... may with

B2: Caption and photographs heading a lengthy and largely inaccurate account of my rescue of Louie May in *Lloyd's Weekly News*, 14 June 1908. *(p 147)*

B3: After my accident I recuperated at Field Farm, near Uttoxeter in Staffordshire. Behind me as I sit in the squire's wheelchair are members of the Hollins family, *left to right:* Frances (the cow-herd), Bill, Mrs Hollins, Jenny, Rupert, Mr Charles Hollins and Becky. *(p 151)*

B4: At Ashby I pose beside my 'solo' balloon, with Captain Gaudron on my right and 'nurse' Becky beside him. On my left is the doctor whom the Captain had brought along 'just in case', and on the extreme right of the group is Mr Shields, who had given me my first ride in a motor car several years earlier. My parachute is laid out ready to be attached to the balloon. *(p 153)*

B5: A later edition of my parachuting outfit. In my right hand I hold the silken Union Jack that I used to wave to the crowds as I ascended under the balloon. On my left wrist is the personal aneroid to indicate my altitude.

B6: Ascending under a hot-air balloon from the Alexandra Palace, holding on to the trapeze bar with one hand and waving to the crowd with the other. This was the occasion when I stood in for a male colleague at the last moment and, being without my normal parachuting costume, had to pin my dress up between my legs. *(p 64)*

B7: Myself with John Turnbull's glider, outside the barn on Box Hill where I helped him with his experiments and made my first and only 'flight' in his machine.

B8: Wolverhampton was the venue for a major Aviation Meeting in 1910. Intentional or not, this postcard cartoon was a sign of the times, for it shows the aeroplane dominating the aerial scene, with the balloon receding in the distance. It was the end of an era. *(p 157)*

Having a High Old Time at Wolverhampton

B9: In the First World War I served as a driver on the Western Front. I am in the centre at the back of this group of driver-mechanics at the MT Depot ASC, Northern Sector (Calais) in 1917. *(p 168)*

B10: Driver Shepherd. "I do not like your face " said the French photographer, "you must come again." Contemplating another sitting, a click and an explosive "Voilà!" assured her it would not be necessary.

B11: In the second World War I served as Shelter Staff Officer for Lewisham in SE London. *(p 171)*

B12: In 1976 I met the Red Devils and actually flew with them when they gave a display in Sussex from their Islander aircraft.
From left to right: Chris Simpson, myself, Barry Grossart, Ian Christie, Dick Kalinski, John Street, Mike Knowles. How different their equipment is from that I used seventy years before! *(p 174)*

B13: *Left* – With Jackie Smith – World Parachuting Champion and member of the Red Devils. *(p 173)*

B14: With the RAF 'Falcons' after they had given a display at Eastbourne in July 1983.
Back row left to right: Al MacDonald, Nigel Rogoff, Jim Hughes, Rex Pritchard, Nick Oswald, Dave Wood, Brian Stevenson, Reg Bayley, Al Chaney.
Front row left to right: Dave Griffiths, Ron Crawford, myself, Dave Hart, Mike Milburn. *(p 176)*

Engulfed in the happy atmosphere of their home whenever I visited them, I soon found myself assisting their practice
and returning their kindness by helping in the dispensary. This
small and spotless room adjoined the surgery and was dominated by three glass containers, with wooden taps at their bases,
holding liquids coloured green, pink and cloudy white. The pink
was 'mist tussi rubra', a special concoction for coughs, colds
and influenza; the green for indigestion and similar conditions,
contained soluble bismuth with peppermint flavouring and
colouring; whilst the cloudy white 'medicine' was nothing more
than a weak solution of Epsom salts flavoured with syrup of
orange!

Dressed in nurse's uniform, it was my allotted job to fill
appropriately labelled bottles with any of the three liquids as
requested by the doctor at the end of each consultation. The
cloudy white was for those with imagined rather than actual
illnesses. Many of the patients swore by it! The dispensing of
the numerous pills and ointments that were also kept in the
room was carried out by the doctor himself. The medicine was
included in the charge of 2s. 0d. per visit.

An interesting feature of that little room was an unglazed
earthenware pan kept on a bench in the corner. It was covered
with muslin, half filled with soft water, and with pebbles, moss
and charcoal at the bottom. It contained leeches. These were
used for reducing inflamed or congested areas. The part to be
'bled' was cleansed and often smeared with a sugar solution
before the leeches were attached. As they sucked the blood and
impurities, they swelled visibly until they could take no more
– and dropped off. A leech could extract about two teaspoon-
fuls of blood, which was then removed from the creatures by
immersing them in a salt solution. Then it was back into the
pan ready to be used again!

Sometimes I would accompany the doctor on his rounds,
when he would visit patients for a charge of 2s. 6d. The landau
would be at his front door promptly at ten-thirty, the coachman
dressed in a long black coat and top hat. The doctor would pick
up his large black bag, fully equipped in case of emergency,

and always ready at the front door. Off we would go at a quick trot, hoping to get finished by lunchtime

Meal times were always interesting, as the couple would discuss the patients, showing great concern for the serious ones, and a light-hearted tolerance towards those with imagined illnesses, for which they always received a sympathetic ear and a bottle of the white 'medicine'. Dr O'Brian was a clever psychologist as well as a skilled family doctor. He was dedicated to his calling, never spared himself and rarely took a holiday. Fortunately, although I made many parachute jumps in the Wolverhampton area, I never had to call on his medical skills myself! The day would come, however, when I would be only too grateful for the attentions of others of his profession...

Occasionally I was fortunate enough to be entertained by members of the upper classes and to taste the luxuries and the gracious living which many people today associate with the Edwardian age but which were in fact limited to a privileged few.

My first encounter with the aristocracy happened early in my parachuting career when I was booked for the August Bank Holiday at Tamworth in 1906. Having made an uneventful 'up-and-downer' nearby on the Monday, Captain Gaudron and I stayed the night at the 'Peel Arms' in order to be on the spot for a performance the next day at Drayton Manor, the home of the famous Peel family. The Captain as usual left early to prepare the balloon, and I spent the morning strolling round the charming little village, until it was time to prepare myself for a visit to the Manor, where it had been arranged for me to meet Sir Robert Peel. For the occasion I wore a fitted silk dress of powder blue, with a short train and long sleeves, a picture hat with feathers and gloves – as always. At two o'clock precisely a horse and carriage drew up outside the hotel, and Mr George, the Steward of the Peel Estates, introduced himself in courteous fashion. He handed me into the carriage, and together we left for Drayton Manor.

Passing through the Swiss Lodge Gate, we entered a long

drive, on either side of which were clusters of rhododendrons flanked by a variety of magnificent trees, offering welcome shade from the heat of the sun. The gentle trickling of water drew attention to the little stream running beneath bridges on one side, while on the other, set in a thicket of trees, was an aviary containing rare birds in gorgeous plumage.

Neither the beauty of the drive nor Mr George's description of the Manor with its seventy-eight rooms prepared me for the unimaginable splendour of the scene that came suddenly into view. It was like a fairy-tale palace! I was awestruck as I descended from the carriage and walked through the magnificent portals into the grandiose hall. Only when I heard myself addressed by name did I realize that this was not a dream and that there, standing before me so tall and elegant, was the handsome figure of Sir Robert Peel. He shook me warmly by the hand and soon put me at my ease as he took me round the main rooms of the Manor, where I relived the history of the past hundred years.

The first Robert Peel had rebuilt the mellow Elizabethan house in 1790. His son – grandfather of the present Sir Robert – had been the great Victorian statesman who had risen to be Prime Minister and had founded the Metropolitan Police Force – known after him as 'Peelers', then as 'Bobbies', and eventually as 'Coppers'.* It had been Robert Peel the statesman who had made the house into this palatial residence which had numbered Queen Victoria and her consort Prince Albert amongst its many distinguished guests.

I was led as though in a trance through the Statesman's Gallery with its portraits and busts of famous political figures; the marble floored conservatory with its exotic flowers; the dining-room modelled on that of Buckingham Palace; the magnificent ballroom; the library; and eventually on to the balustraded terraces overlooking the Italian gardens ablaze with geraniums and with numerous pools surmounted by fountains.

*'Coppers' because they would parade twelve at a time before going on their beat, there being twelve coppers (pennies) to a bob (one shilling).

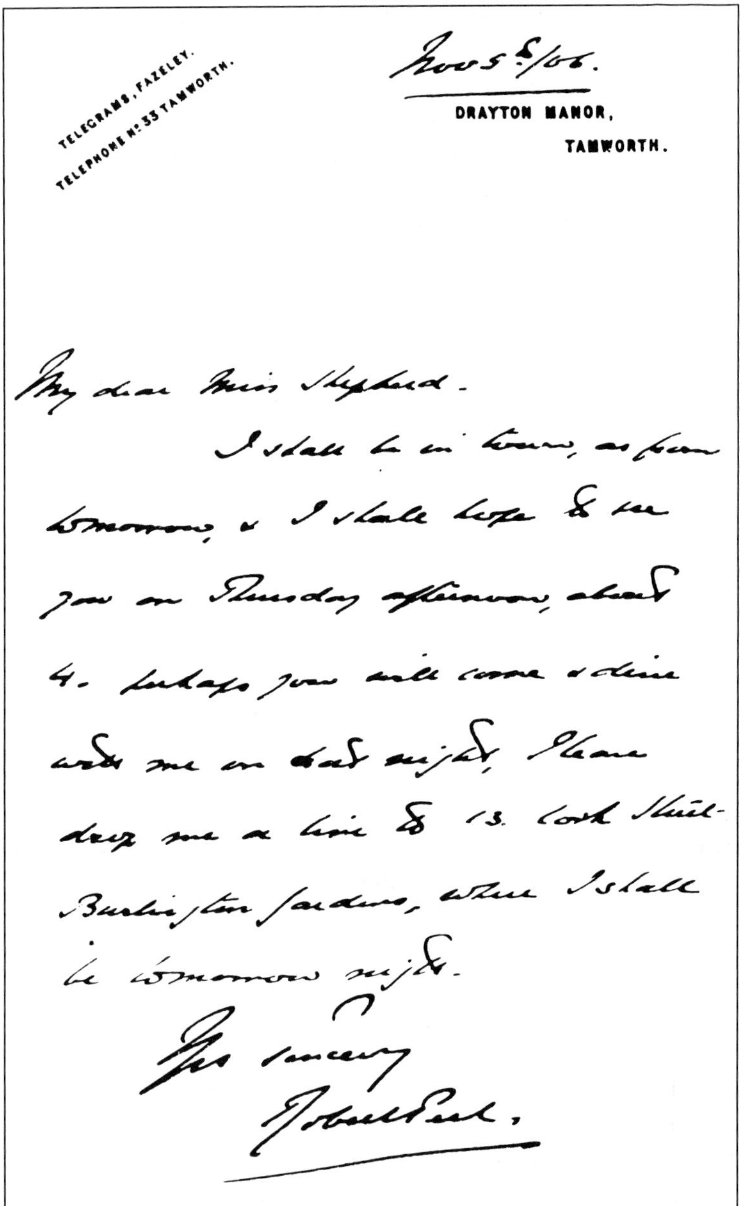

TELEGRAMS, FAZELEY.
TELEPHONE N°35 TAMWORTH.

Nov 5ᵗʰ/06.

DRAYTON MANOR,

TAMWORTH.

My dear Miss Shepherd.

I shall be in town, as from tomorrow, & I shall hope to see you on Thursday afternoon, about 4. Perhaps you will come & dine with me on that night, Please drop me a line to 13. South Street Burlington Gardens, where I shall be tomorrow night.

Yrs sincerely

Robert Peel,

Sir Robert Peel's invitation

Beyond stretched the velvety lawns, the woodlands and the park with its avenues of stately Himalayan pines.

Returning to the drawing room, Sir Robert announced that we would have tea before meeting a number of his friends. Seeing that I was comfortably seated, he walked over to where there hung a thick silken cord ending in a tassel. He had barely pulled it when the double doors opened and a footman in full livery appeared: blue velvet breeches, white silken hose and black patent shoes with buckles.

"Tea, please," said Sir Robert in a gentle tone.

Almost instantaneously a table was wheeled in, set out with glittering silver, fine china and dainty morsels. Whilst we chatted over tea, Sir Robert asked if there was anything special I would like to do or see before I left. There was one thing that I very much wanted to do.

"I know it sounds silly," I said, "but I would love to pull that cord."

"So you shall," he replied with a smile. "I see we have no chocolate cake. Would you like to order some?"

Feeling very important, I crossed to the silken cord and pulled it. Like the genie in *Aladdin and the Lamp* the liveried footman appeared.

"Will you please bring some chocolate cake," said Sir Robert in his usual courteous manner. The footman left, to reappear as if by magic with the chocolate cake, which was placed on the table and duly sampled.

Conversation flowed easily and turned naturally to parachuting, then to the evening's event. Seeing that I was now more at ease, Sir Robert suggested that it was time to meet his friends. I was accustomed to meeting people, but not a room full of the aristocracy! I took a deep breath and followed my host into the reception room. To my great relief a comely and charming lady came forward with outstretched arms and with a kiss on the cheek said, "Oh, how lovely to see you, Miss Shepherd!"

This kindly gesture by a duchess put me completely at ease, so that I was able to mingle happily with the other guests and to answer their many questions. What was it like, coming down in a parachute? Wasn't it terribly dangerous? Why did I do it? They were the same questions that were put to me by the butcher boys and housemaids at any show!

At about five o'clock, and feeling a little like Cinderella, I left to change into my parachuting outfit, then made my way to the balloon enclosure on the lawns. It was already encircled by a large crowd of country folk, and as I chatted to them I found that many had come to the fête by special trains from the more distant villages and towns.

There was no gas supply available, so we were to use the hot-air balloon. Its preparation had caused the usual interest, and when it was almost ready, the Captain joined me in my friendly discussion with the specatators, for on this occasion we were to make a double descent. I noticed that Sir Robert and his friends had come out on to the terrace, where the Band of the Kettering Rifles was still playing.

As soon as the balloon was fully inflated and was standing up without the aid of its poles, we checked our parachutes and took up our positions. The Captain gave the command, the men holding the smoky balloon stepped back smartly as they let go, and we trotted forward a few paces until the rising bag swept us from the ground. We responded happily to the cheering crowds, with a special wave to the distinguished gathering on the terrace as we soared into the bright blue sky.

How beautiful the Manor looked from on high! It was a gem, set in green velvet, with its ponds and fountains sparkling prettily around it. It was so different from the industrial landscapes that I so often gazed down on from these Midland skies. Everything was so orderly, and verdant – so rich.

As we swung side by side in space about two thousand feet above the enchanting scene, the usual argument began as to when to pull away, but I didn't prolong it as much as I normally would under a gas balloon, for the life of the hot air was limited, and I had no wish for that big black bag to collapse on top of me. So at 2,500 feet I obediently pulled away, with the Captain following almost immediately, and the balloon coming down after us with its usual belch of black smoke as it was unceremoniously upended.

Weather conditions being ideal, our descents were perfect and in full view of the delighted spectators. We both landed near the Bleach Works at Bonehill and together were driven back to an enthusiastic reception at the manor grounds.

As we were discussing our performance with Sir Robert's guests, there was sudden consternation on the terrace. Sir Robert's seven-year-old son was missing. In a few moments he was discovered on the edge of one of the pools, grasping a big black umbrella. He was brought back to his father, who asked what he had been up to. The little lad explained that he had been jumping from one of the terraces with the umbrella – just like Miss Shepherd!

The sequel to this pleasant episode at Drayton Manor came a few months later when Sir Robert invited me to dinner at the Berkeley Hotel. Aunty, who always kept a very tight rein on my association with gentlemen, for once allowed me to go. What an adventure for a young girl! I dressed for the occasion in a black evening dress, under a black velvet coat with fur collar. The Berkeley was one of the grandest hotels in London, and I felt far more nervous in its magnificent foyer than I had ever felt in a balloon enclosure! However, Sir Robert soon put me at my ease with his charming manner and pleasant conversation – although I remained somewhat dismayed by an array of cutlery and glasses such as I had never seen before! Sir Robert had brought his steward with him to act as chaperon and to ensure propriety, though I was never quite sure whom he was there to protect – me or Sir Robert.

How sad to recall that the famous Peel family and Drayton Manor are no more. Sir Robert died in 1925 at the age of fifty-eight. Young Bobbie-of-the-umbrella married the well-known actress Beatrice Lillie in 1920 but died in 1934. His only son Robert was killed at the age of twenty-one when the destroyer *HMS Tenedos* went down off Ceylon in 1942. With the passing of the last of the Peel family, the tenant farmers at Drayton Manor had been able to buy their land, and the complete estate was sold off. Alas, in the 1949 'Sale of the Century' there were no bidders for the Manor itself, and the magnificent building that had impressed me so much was levelled to the ground. There were rumours that the stones had been sent to America. Where that monument to gracious living once stood, there is now a pleasure park and a zoo!

My relationship with Sir Robert was no more than a passing friendship, of course, but a number of gentlemen with whom I became acquainted through my parachuting showed more serious intentions, and I received several offers of marriage. The main obstacle that my suitors faced was Aunty. She was very protective at the best of times, and if the gentleman in question should in any way be connected with my parachuting, then he stood no chance at all! Harry Hassle, for instance, was a charming and wealthy young man whom I met at Ashby and who subsequently pursued me to London, although I had advised him not to. When he presented himself to my aunt in the showroom of the Feather Emporium and asked if he might take me to the theatre, her reply was immediate and emphatic.

"No," she said, "I don't want anything to do with her parachuting capers."

Harry couldn't believe his ears. He was quite furious. Without saying a word, he walked round the showroom in dignified manner and, with his silver topped cane, deliberately burst each of the new electric lights that we had just had installed. Then he dropped a £5 note in front of my astonished aunt and stalked out! He later wrote me an apology, and we used to laugh about it whenever I met him after that, for I continued to see him during my periodic visits to Ashby and Derby. I am afraid that Aunty's over-protective attitude forced me to conduct several of my friendships without her knowledge.

Another of my suitors met with a little more success than Harry. One day when I went with Aunty to the Alexandra Palace, we seemed to meet this tall, elegant figure wherever we turned. He had the appearance and bearing of someone of note and was accompanied by a short man who looked like a private detective – as indeed he proved to be. When we bumped into the handsome stranger yet again, we couldn't help but smile at each other, at which he raised his hat and asked if he could have my address. He obviously knew who I was, having probably seen one of my performances.

Aunty's response was quite predictable. "No, certainly not!" she said sternly. She turned and beckoned a cab, and away we drove.

When we arrived home and the four-wheeler came to a halt, the door was opened for us – by the handsome stranger! He and his companion had hopped on to the bar at the rear of the cab as it had driven away! Such initiative appealed to Aunty's sense of humour, so that she relented and actually let me go to dinner with our mysterious gentleman – with his detective dining at a separate table. I came to know him as Paul Stein, though I am not sure if that really was his name. He was Hungarian, very wealthy and oh, so elegant in his dinner suit, opera hat and black cape lined with red silk! He subsequently asked me to marry him, but I declined. I didn't fancy Hungary.

Such were the pleasures and advantages of being an Edwardian lady parachutist! So many friends, from all walks of life; so many opportunities to *do* things; so many exciting experiences; so many happy landings.

Yet most attractive of all to me was the sheer exhilaration and joy that I found in the air. I never lost that sense of wonderment and ecstasy whenever I floated alone in the awesome silence of the infinite skies. Every ascent renewed in me those same feelings of delight and contentment. When I soared upwards, above all earthly worries and discomforts, my mind was set free to wander at will and to absorb the sensations of gentle flight, and the beauty of everything around and below me. I never failed to marvel at my bird's eye view of the scenes below, where rural or urban, forming an intricately woven tapestry above which I floated so effortlessly. In those days, flight in any form was an experience known only to a very few of us. Remember – no aeroplane flew in England until 1908, when Cody managed a short hop into the air. Before that, the air belonged to us with our balloons and parachutes – to a handful of showmen and sportsmen and to those with enough courage and money to take a flight as a passenger. We were a privileged few.

Yes, it was the lure of the skies and the unique thrills of ascent and descent that held me to this strange calling – and that were to entice me back even after it came very close to claiming my life yet again...

Drayton Manor

8

The First Mid-Air Rescue

Throughout the years that I was parachuting, my aunt and I kept to the agreement that we had made before my very first descent at the Alexandra Palace. I would tell her when I had an engagement for a show and how long I would be away, but would say nothing more about it before or afterwards. Naturally I was sorry that she and Uncle Will thought so poorly of what they called my 'mountebank stunts', for I would love to have shared my pleasures and experiences with them. Nor were there many opportunities to discuss my parachuting adventures with my parents. Although Mum and Dad raised no objections, they were of course concerned for my safety, and I always made a point of sending them a telegram from my various shows to let them know that I was all right. Sometimes, because it was more convenient to do so, I sent the telegram *before* the show!

Having a young girl's natural urge to share experiences with others, I used to relate the details of my parachuting escapades to the other girls in the Ostrich Feather Emporium where I worked for Aunty throughout this time.

The Emporium was in Theobalds Road in Holborn, on the site where the Ministry of Defence now has offices. It comprised a shop front, a showroom and various workrooms occupying three floors and a basement, all dedicated to the conversion of raw ostrich feathers into the magnificent plumes that decorated dresses, hats, stoles and boas of that period of great elegance.

The manufacturing process was long and irksome. The feathers came from South Africa and Egypt in their raw state.

And very raw it was! First of all each feather had to be scraped to remove its root – a really dirty job known as 'pething'. They would then be soaked in a solution of silicate of soda for a day to remove the grease and sand, then washed in soap and water and rinsed. Next they would be 'beaten out' to dry them, which was again hard and dirty work usually reserved for the apprentices. To bleach them they would be soaked in a vat of peroxide and ammonia. After further washing and rinsing, they would be ready for dyeing. Following this they would be beaten out and steamed, and then 'laid up' preparatory to invisible sewing. When the articles had been made up, they would be steamed and 'fired', a warming and drying process, and finally curled – a very intricate and exacting task – to complete the transformation into plumes of extraordinary beauty.

When Aunty had taken me on to learn the trade – as an alternative to a life of sin on the stage, you will remember – she had insisted that I should start at the bottom with the 'pething' and work my way right through the various jobs until I was competent in all of them. It usually took the girls from one to two years to finish such an apprenticeship, but Aunty saw to it that I completed mine in six months.

Aunty was a fair but quite formidable mistress. The first thing that the girls would ask me in the morning was, "Miss Doll, how's the Missus got her hair done?" If it was soft and wavy, it would be a pleasant day, but if it was severely pulled back and done with a bun on top, then trouble would be brewing! When she opened a retail shop in Leicester Square and moved across to manage it herself, she put me in charge at the Emporium. The girls probably thought that they were in for an easier time, but they soon learnt from experience that I too could be firm. In the dyeing-room downstairs we had large five-gallon vats for the colouring process, and on one occasion when we had finished dyeing a quantity of brown feathers, I noticed that one of the girls was sitting on the edge of one of the vats.

"Get off, Lottie," I said.

She didn't move. Again, more firmly, I said, "Lottie, get off. If you don't, I'll push you in."

She sat there defiantly. So I pushed her in. I didn't have any bother after that!

They were good girls, with tremendous spirit and not afraid of hard work. They took a great pride in their craftsmanship, as so many people did in those days. We worked from half-past-eight in the morning until eight o'clock at night, with forty-five minutes for lunch, when they would send out for $1\frac{1}{2}$d. worth of fish and chips known as 'a penny and a' porth', or a hunk of bread and a quarter pound of cheese for $1\frac{1}{2}$d. To relieve the tedium of the long day, we would sing as we worked, often from the scores of the musical comedies that were so popular. With the money that I earned from my parachuting I sometimes took the girls to the theatre, usually to the operettas, for 9d each in the gallery. I often bought little gifts for them too, either personal things or household articles. Yes, there was plenty of jollity, despite the hard work.

Each time that I returned from a parachuting display, the girls were eager to hear every detail of my adventures. Most of them shared the view that they wouldn't do such a thing for love nor money, but there was one notable exception. Her name was Louie May.

Louie worked in the showroom. She was an attractive girl of medium height, with an abundance of fair hair and big blue eyes. She became so enraptured with my accounts of the thrills and pleasures of the air that she decided she would like to try them for herself and begged for an opportunity to make a descent. She was a strong girl with bags of spirit, so I mentioned her to Captain Gaudron. He interviewed her, gave her the same half-hour of training that I had undergone and to her great delight said that he would take her on as soon as an opportunity arose.

It came sooner than we expected. I had been double-booked for a show at Ashby and a two-day event at Longton in June 1908. Ashby was to be a solo descent, but at Longton it was a jump from the basket of a 'right-away' balloon – a 'beginner's jump', which Louie could do. So the Captain asked her to fulfil the engagement for the first day at Longton, and she was delighted to accept.

There was one snag: her fiancé. On no account must he – or her grandmother with whom she was living – get to hear of the escapade, or they would certainly forbid it. It had to be a closely guarded secret, so she told them that she was going away with a girlfriend for the weekend. I shared both her secret and her excitement, for I could remember how I had felt before my own first descent some four years earlier.

As planned, Louie left with Captain Gaudron for Longton, and I went to Ashby, to be greeted by the many friends I had made there in the course of previous visits. The day of the show was fine, and despite a stiff breeze the ascent and the descent were both without incident and fully successful. As I bundled up my parachute after landing, I wondered how Louie had got on.

After being entertained to dinner, I took the train to Longton, arriving just before midnight. I asked the first porter I saw if he had been to the show and if the parachute descent had gone off well.

"There wasn't one," he said with a disappointed shrug of his shoulders.

Perplexed and anxious, I made arrangements to leave my packed balloon and parachute at the station, then hurried to the hotel, where the Captain was waiting for me.

"Whatever happened?" I asked him.

With a despairing gesture he said, "It was too windy for her to jump, so I wouldn't let her go. We pulled her back into the basket, and she came with us for the rest of the flight."

Poor Louie! To have prepared herself for that first fearful leap into space, only to be thwarted at the last moment! I could imagine how disappointed she must have felt. But the chance to make that first descent had been delayed by only one day, for the Captain had decided that, to compensate the crowds for their disappointment, Louie would jump with me the following afternoon.

"You will both jump from the basket," he said, "and I want you to go out early and show yourself to the people, for they were very sorry that you were not here today."

The next morning was bright and warm, and fortunately the wind had gone somewhere else. It was ideal for the show. Despite her disappointment of the previous day, Louie was in good spirits as we mingled with the gathering crowds. There was considerable excitement amongst them as the news spread that there was to be a double descent.

An added attraction at this particular show was the appearance of Gaudron's *Mammoth* balloon, at that time the largest ever to be built in Britain, made of 1,482 panels of varnished cotton with a capacity of nearly 108,000 cubic feet. It was in this giant balloon that the Captain had recently set a new British long-distance record. With Captain Maitland and Charles Turner as passengers, he had ascended from Crystal Palace into a strong westerly airflow that had carried them over Berlin within seventeen hours, and onwards towards Russia. As darkness had enveloped them, they had encountered intense cold and a violent snowstorm. The *Mammoth* became increasingly difficult to control, and they were forced to descend until the sound of the wind roaring through unseen trees in the blackness below warned them that they were close to the ground. Gaudron had waited until the last moment before he pulled the ripping cord. They landed with a tremendous crash, not in trees as expected but on an open stretch of ice and snow, across which the basket was dragged and bumped at great speed, with its passengers hanging on for dear life. They came to a halt at last on the very edge of a lake, all thoroughly shaken and Gaudron with a gashed forehead. Their troubles were not quite over, for the Russian peasants and officials who were eventually contacted took them for spies! When their credentials were at last established, they found that they had landed near the town of Abelar in the Russian province of Novo Alexandrovsk, having covered a distance of 1,150 miles from the Crystal Palace.

The *Mammoth* (sometimes called *Graphic* after the epic journey to Russia, sponsored by the newspaper of that name) and Captain Gaudron's record-breaking flight for which he was awarded the annual Gold Medal by the Aero Club of the United Kingdom were major topics of conversation as Louie and I chatted with the people gathered round the enclosure to watch the preparations. Excitement rose as the majestic balloon became an enormous, netted orb of silver, glistening in the sunlight and standing supreme, like a resplendent goddess with her subjects clustered about her.

Suddenly, black clouds obscured the sun. We had all been so busy watching the balloon that we had not noticed them gathering silently in the sky. A few moments later there was a short but heavy downpour of rain. The goddess quivered, wavered, staggered... she gave a long sigh, and her regal figure began gradually to collapse. The stark reality stunned the spectators. They let out an involuntary groan as the truth dawned on them. The *Mammoth* was deflating.

"No smoking! No smoking!" went up the cry.

"NO SMOKING PLEASE. GAS IS ESCAPING!" boomed a louder voice over a megaphone to the panicking crowd.

The spectators moved quickly away from the enclosure, to continue watching from a distance, leaving Captain Gaudron and his team in utter dismay. It looked as though another show was going to be cancelled. How disappointed the public would be! And Louie – to have her hopes dashed a second time! But the Captain had no intention of letting the spectators down again.

Turning to me he said, "Did you bring your balloon back with you?"

"Yes," I replied, "I left it at the station."

"Then we'll use it. You can make a double descent from that. We'll have it brought from the station straight away."

A pony and trap were despatched in haste. Whilst we waited for it to return with my solo balloon, the Captain overhauled the *Mammoth* to see what had caused it to deflate. He discovered that the top valve had been slightly ruptured. Willing hands helped him to fold the sad balloon and pack it into its basket.

As soon as my balloon arrived from the station, the gas pipe was attached, and inflation began without delay. Although it needed only twenty thousand cubic feet of gas, filling it would still be a lengthy process. Louie and I mixed once more with the crowd, whose hopes and interest had been renewed by the announcement that a double descent *would* take place, not from the basket but from under the balloon. It was well into the evening before the little princess stood there, perky but proud, in the space previously occupied by the majestic goddess, nearly five times her size.

My parachute was attached to the balloon by the usual ring and cotter pin, customary for a solo descent. To attach Louie's 'chute, however, the Captain had to improvise a similar mechanism. It worked perfectly well when he tested it there on the ground. As was usual in a double ascent, a thick cord was attached to the bar of one parachute – in this case Louie's – whilst I held the free end. This would provide a link between us during the ascent and would help us to avoid entanglement as we swung in mid-air, about six to eight feet apart.

We gave our 'chutes a final check. After the previous disappointments, the excitement of the crowd grew to a crescendo as, just before eight o'clock, we stepped into our respective slings. I gave a final word of encouragement to Louie and gave the order to let go. Together we ran forward beneath the rising balloon, to be lifted smoothly into the air alongside each other. I responded to the jubilant cheers with a wave of my silken Union Jack as we soared effortlessly into the still air of the evening.

Louie showed no fear. Just as I had been on my first ascent, she was entranced by the toy-town aspect of the scene below us and by the silence and stillness of the skies.

"I wouldn't have missed this for *anything!*' she called to me as we swung gently in space. "It really is exhilarating."

Our ride into the sky was smooth and uneventful, and all too soon it was time for us to return to the distant earth. I spotted a clear space for our landing.

"Well, we're touching on three thousand feet," I said. "How do you feel? Are you ready to pull away?"

"I'm fine," she replied happily. "I know now why you

always enjoyed your trips! All right – I'll pull away now."

I prepared to let go of the line that connected us as I watched Louie reach for her liberating cord. She gave it a sharp pull.

Nothing happened.

"Try again, but pull harder," I called.

Once again she pulled and tugged, but still she remained firmly attached to the balloon.

"What shall I do?" she called. "I can't get away."

"Don't panic. Try once more."

I watched in growing dismay as she continued to tug at the cord – and continued to hang there alongside me. It was obvious that something had gone wrong with the release mechanism. All the time the balloon was soaring upwards, getting closer and closer to the gathering clouds. We were at about eight thousand feet. My mind was working feverishly as I recalled the time when I had been unable to separate from the balloon, and the problem I had faced then. I had to make Louie hang on, just as I had done.

Trying to sound more cheerful than I felt, I called across to her, "Hang on, Louie! Whatever you do – hang on! The gas will seep out and we shall come down eventually."

"Have you ever had difficulty in getting away before?" she asked.

"Well... yes, I have. But I came down all right." I didn't tell her that it had taken more than three hours for me to come down. Could she hold on for that long? Perhaps I should do something now, rather than just hang there, waiting...

I still had hold of the cord that joined us, and used it now to pull us together. I reached over and took Louie's liberating cord and gave it a sharp pull myself. It was a foolhardy thing to do, I realized afterwards, for had she fallen away then, she would probably have dragged me with her, or her 'chute might have twined itself round mine. My attempt to free her was to no avail, however, and I let her swing back again.

"Just hang on! We should soon start coming down," I tried to reassure her.

Suddenly we were wrapped in a cold fog. Clouds. This

was all too familiar to me! I could see Louie swinging there like some ghostly figure, wreathed in mist. We soon broke though the cloud and into light, which I thought might hearten her. It had quite the opposite effect. When she looked down and realized that the earth had completely disappeared and that there was only a thick carpet of cloud below, she showed fear for the first time. She said nothing, but I could see the terror in her face and in her eyes and in the tension in her body as she clung desperately to the trapeze bar.

"Look *up*, Louie," I called out. "Don't look down. Keep looking *up*."

I glanced at my aneroid. We were almost at eleven thousand feet and still rising. The air was now very chill. My anxiety grew, not for myself but for my companion. Suppose her hands became numb with the cold? Suppose she lost her will to hold on? How much longer before we started to come down?

I could have pulled away and saved myself at any time, but the thought never occurred to me. I was responsible for Louie, and there was no question of leaving her. It was not a conscious nor a brave decision. It was the only thing to do.

Another look at Louie and I knew that we could not wait for the balloon to tire. There she hung, a limp figure hanging grimly on to life, but her face was deathly white, her lips blue with cold, her eyes wide open and staring with suppressed fear. I had to act *now*. There was only one thing to do. Somehow I would have to take her down with me. We would have to entrust ourselves to a single parachute. I knew that it would be a terrible risk, but there was no alternative. She could not hold on much longer, and we had to use her remaining strength while it lasted.

"Louie, you're very plucky," I called out, trying to encourage her – trying to give her heart for the frightening and difficult task ahead. "Don't worry, I won't leave you. I've made up my mind – you're coming down on my parachute."

I realized how small my voice must have sounded in the immensity of that vast aerial hall in which we floated so helplessly, and I tried to sharpen it to persuade Louie that I was well in control, and confident of the outcome.

"Now – do as I tell you," I commanded. "As I pull the cord, you swing over to me... Good!"

We were face to face, holding on to each other's bar with one hand, and to our respective trapeze bars with the other. I crooked one arm round the cords of both parachutes, then grasped my bar again with both hands, thus holding us together. Now for the most perilous part of the operation – transferring Louie from one parachute to the other, with a two-mile drop waiting below us for the slightest slip.

"Now we must get your belt off."

Each using one hand, clinging tightly to the trapeze bar with the other, we frantically pulled and tugged, until at last the safety belt was released.

"Now... hold my bar with one hand and keep holding yours with the other... Right! Take your legs out of the sling and put them round my waist, one at a time... That's it!"

I tried to keep my voice calm. Tried to keep the fear from it. Tried to make it sound as though I were asking her to do something quite easy – while my mind was racing ahead, trying to work out an instant solution to a formidable problem. How best to put her hands? On my bar? Round my neck?

Her legs tightened round my waist like a vice.

"Now... transfer your other hand to *my* bar... Good!"

I let go of her empty parachute, which swung away to hang free and useless alongside us. We were now committed to the single 'chute.

Seconds counted now. I had to pull away, but I couldn't reach the ripping-cord.

"Louie – you'll have to put your arms round my neck. Now... one at a time."

I felt the full weight of her body suddenly dragging on mine as she entrusted herself entirely to me, and I prayed that my arms would hold us both – that the sling would take our combined weight. Would the parachute open? Or would our weight be too much for it? Would the sling hold? Would our strength last? The thoughts flashed through my mind as I contemplated the ripping-cord that would send us plummeting

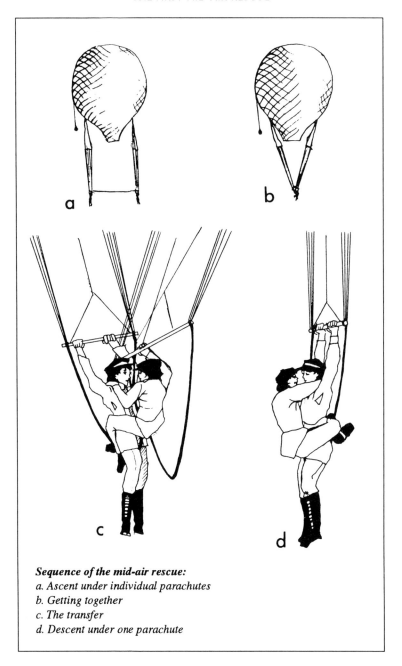

Sequence of the mid-air rescue:
a. Ascent under individual parachutes
b. Getting together
c. The transfer
d. Descent under one parachute

earthwards.

"If you've never said a prayer before, say one now," I gasped.

"And hold tightly... I'm going to pull away... NOW!"

Praying that the release pin would not be jammed by the extra load on the parachute, I jerked hard on the cord with my right hand. Instantly we were falling. My companion gave a sharp cry and her grip on me tightened convulsively as we hurtled through the air, waiting those endless seconds for the 'chute to open. I could hear the silk streaming and rippling above us, and craned my head back to look up at it as it struggled for life. Slowly... slowly it blossomed... but not completely. The silken dome was in some way mis-shapen. It was not fully open, but enough to arrest our breath-taking plunge.

"We're all right, Louie! We're all right! The 'chute has opened... just hang on now... just hang on..." I panted, trying to reassure her, although I knew that our troubles were far from over. We were dropping too fast under the incomplete canopy, and we were still above cloud. What lay below it? Town or countryside? Fields or forest?

The speed with which the woolly carpet suddenly came up to envelope us told me that we were falling much too fast. To hit the ground at that speed would be fatal. Holding on for dear life – she to me, and me to the bar – we came through the clouds and into the light once more. To my relief there was open countryside spread below us.

I felt a slight pull on the trapeze bar. Looking up, I saw that the parachute had taken a second breath and that the canopy had assumed its proper and very beautiful proportions. What a welcome sight that was! Even so, I could sense that we were still descending rapidly, and knew that I would be unable to do anything to guide us towards a soft landing-spot.

And so, with Louie clinging desperately to me – it was all happening so quickly that I don't know how – we came swinging down out of the sky under a single parachute. The earth came up fast, as though anxious to welcome us back. I was aware of a road rushing towards us and gave an involuntary cry.

"Oh no! Please... not that!"

The next moment we crashed to the ground, six feet short of the road and narrowly missing a scythe stuck in the soil! I threw myself backwards, and Louie, still twined round my body like a vine, bounced heavily on top of me. The impact of the landing was like a hammer blow.

Louie scrambled immediately to her feet, with a loud cry of alarm. "Oh, all my teeth are out!"

They weren't, of course. We both burst out laughing – an hysterical outburst to relieve the tension.

As Louie rose to her feet, I remained where I was, lying on my back on the ground. I could feel no pain, but something was telling me not to try to leap to my feet with the very joy of being alive. Something was telling me to lie very still. Something was telling me that I was badly hurt.

Within seconds, the rotund figure of a farmer appeared, followed by his wife and children, then another farmer and his family. They offered to help me to my feet, but instinctively, like an injured animal, I knew that I must lie still.

"No – don't touch me!" I cried out. "I need a doctor."

One of the farmers, Charles Hollins, took charge of the situation and sent Mr Horsefell of Shelton off on a bicycle to fetch the doctor, and when I expressed my concern that Captain Gaudron must be told that we had landed, he despatched Mr Goodwin of Longton to the station at Leigh to send off a telegram.

By now a small crowd had gathered. We could hardly understand them on account of their broad local accents, but we learned that we had landed at Field Farm, three miles from Leigh and fourteen from Longton. Someone produced a rug and covered me with it. Louie sat down beside me, and we were given hot drinks. She was shocked but apparently uninjured.

"Well, Dolly, I *have* made a parachute descent," she said. "But why didn't you leave me?"

"You ought to know me better than that!" I retorted. "And thank goodness you're all right. Anyway, we did make a double descent after all, and on *one* parachute. That's a record!"

I heard the sound of a pony and trap on the road, and the group that was gathered around us made way for the newcomer, who was soon on this knees beside me. It was the doctor.

"How do you feel?" he asked.

"I just want the earth dug away – and let me fall through," I replied.

I was having difficulty forming my words. Something was happening to my mouth, as though it were being pulled and twisted by invisible wires.

"I'm afraid she has damaged her back. I'll want a stretcher, or anything firm would do," I heard the doctor say as he rose from his brief examination.

A few minutes later I was being gently lifted on to a door which the resourceful Mr Hollins had taken off its hinges. I was carried carefully to his house, and whilst an improvised fracture bed was being prepared for me, I was placed on the floor at the foot of the staircase. The bedroom was occupied by two youngsters who had to be roused from sleep. Drowsily they came down the stairs in their nightshirts, and as they stepped over me I could see quite plainly that they were boys!

When the bed was ready, I was carried up the stairs and laid upon it. My body was found to be twisted, and it was suggested that my clothes should be cut away, but the farmer's thrifty and practically minded wife contrived, with her daughters, to ease them off.

Everything was becoming rather vague now. The pain was not great, but as the doctor examined me I could sense those invisible wires pulling tighter and tighter at my mouth until it became fixed in a one-sided grimace, and I could no longer speak. Everything seemed unreal. I was close to unconsciousness. I was dimly aware of whispered conversations; of concerned faces looking down at me; of someone talking of brandy and milk; of Captain Gaudron expressing his sympathy and assuring me that he would take Louie back to London in the morning; then quietness and the dim light of the oil lamp and the comfort of someone sitting silently beside the bed...

For the next three days I hovered between unconsciousness and a vague awareness of what was going on around me. For much of the time I slept, and whenever I opened my eyes a feeding-cup with brandy and milk was forced into the corner of my still-fixed mouth. I was dimly aware of the visits by the doctor and a colleague, but not of the reporters who besieged the house, nor the endless stream of people bringing flowers and good wishes. I was not even aware of the visit by my mother. I was never left alone in the room. Always when I opened my eyes there was a friendly face smiling down at me – the refined features and kind blue eyes of Mrs Hollins herself; the plump, rosy face of Jenny, her eldest daughter; the peaches-and-cream complexion and long fair hair of the younger, Becky; or the smiling faces of Daisy and May Ball, daughters of another local farmer. Night and day there were two of my devoted 'nurses' with me, and every time I woke, there was the inevitable brandy and milk.

By the fourth day, although I was still very drowsy, the doctor and his colleague had decided that I now had every chance of survival and that I was strong enough to stand the pain of being straightened. By now my mouth was beginning to loosen, and a knotted handkerchief was wedged between my teeth to prevent me biting my tongue. With my legs held firmly, the doctors then proceeded to pull my body back into its normal position, straightening my twisted spine. The pain was excruciating, and when the ordeal was over, brandy and milk were called for.

Brandy had been unknown in the Hollins household, and several bottles had been kindly provided by Squire Phillips. Now the two doctors watched in stunned silence as the 'nurse' measured out a tumbler full of brandy and a dash of milk. She poured this into the feeding-cup and handed it to the still-gaping doctor. Then they both burst into laughter.

"Now I can understand why she slept so much!" he said with a grin.

No wonder that things had seemed rather vague to me – I had been drunk for three days!

From then on, with much more milk and a lot less brandy, I soon regained my senses, and also recovered my voice as the paralysis left my mouth. I improved rapidly, but I was still bedridden, yellow from the waist down, and with no feeling in my legs. The family were highly amused by the pin-pricking sessions by which the doctor established this fact. Fortunately my arms were not affected, so that I was able to feed myself and enjoy the good, nutritious country fare that was so lovingly provided for me.

I was able to take more note of my surroundings – to enjoy the profusion of flowers that made the small, cosy room resemble a florist's, and to read and re-read the stack of letters and cards from a multitude of well-wishers. There were numerous visitors to the farm, but few were allowed to see me. One who did was Dr Allen, the Hollins' family doctor, a witty Scot with a strong accent and a tremendous sense of humour that would have me in peals of laughter. He was real tonic so that I always looked forward to his frequent visits.

An exciting moment arrived when it was decided that I was well enough to be taken down to lie in the sun. Arrangements were made through the Squire to borrow a spinal carriage, which was commonly used in those days for invalids with back injuries. When this six-foot long, black-sided box arrived in my room, I was not amused.

"Coo, I thought I was getting better!" I said. "It looks like a coffin!"

I was lifted into it, placed on a fitted mattress and carried gently downstairs, where the box was placed on its four-wheeled iron frame, with handle attached. I was then pushed out into the courtyard where I was able to bask comfortably in the sun and watch everything that was going on around me. I lay there contentedly, thinking how lucky I was to be in this friendly atmosphere and to be looked upon as one of the family. All was quiet, and there I was, soliloquizing peacefully, when the sound of hooves gradually penetrated my thoughts. I was suddenly startled to find two large eyes like balls of velvet peering down at me, growing as large as saucers as they came to within inches of my face. Then, with a low mooing, my unexpected visitor passed on her unhurried way to the milking-shed. Lying there, unable to move, I was petrified until, as the visitors became more numerous, I realized that they were harmless and really quite friendly. With the last of the herd of sixty-nine cows which clopped, lolloped and pushed their way through the yard came the diminutive and impish figure of a nine-year-old girl, happily swinging a stick as she drove her charges to be milked. As she came to the stretcher-bed, she stood and laughed at the obvious uneasiness that her cows had caused.

"Hi, owd Doll – were you fashed?"

"I certainly was!" I replied. "Fancy not warning me, Frances!"

The family were highly amused, but the next day the stretcher-bed was moved so that the homecoming of the cows could be watched from a safer distance.

By now I was allowed a few more visitors, who included my father and a number of reporters who continued to call long after the accident to see how I was progressing, and for friendly chats.

During the next ten days or so, the loving care that I was given conspired with the health-giving rays of the sun and the country air to revitalize and strengthen me, but still I was unable to move my legs. My doctor had explained the extent of my injuries to me. The impact of the landing had caused concussion of the pelvis and spinal paralysis. At least I had been straightened out without aggravating the injuries, but it was too early to judge what the outcome would be. I was beginning to get impatient to be up and going about my normal life – and in particular to get up into the air again. Naturally I often dwelt on the circumstances of that terrifying experience with Louie, and shuddered when I thought what I had asked her to do on her very first descent. For myself, I was determined that I would jump again. I saw no reason why not, although there were a number of people who did. As was always the case after a parachutist was killed or seriously injured, there were many exaggerated and over-sensational reports in the newspapers, and much protest against this form of entertainment – usually from people who knew little about it. A columnist in the *Staffordshire Sentinel* wrote thus:

'We were all glad that the Longton Park Fêtes were financially and as a holiday attraction so successful: but I don't think that parachute descents will form a feature of these occasions in the Potteries for some time to come, at least. Everybody admires the pluck of the two girls who found themselves in such difficulties in mid air and who both behaved with remarkable grit and heroism. Popular sympathy is also very strong with Miss Shepherd who was injured in the descent. No blame attaches to the promoters of the Fêtes. They provided an entertainment which was customary, and no doubt large numbers of people looked forward to it with the greatest possible interest. But Tuesday night's experience shows that parachuting is attended by terrible risk and the public conscience hereabouts has got such a fright that Fête Committees will scarce venture, I think, to put this particular item in their programmes again, just yet. Both girls might easily have been killed and it is a mercy that they escaped. It is not a responsibility that can be lightly entertained."

Notice the 'at least' and the 'just yet'! The writer – and the readers too – knew full well that public curiosity would soon overcome 'public conscience' and that parachuting *would* be back in the Potteries after a decorous interval. There were few who would go as far as the Reverend Edmund Pigott, Vicar of Trentham, in is condemnation of parachuting, also voiced in the *Staffordshire Sentinel*:

'There is nothing in parachute work that justifies the risk that it necessarily entails. Probably to the performer there is great exhilaration in the momentary art of liberating himself and in the extremely rapid passage through the air, and as long as people will pay them in the great fight for livelihood there will never be a lack of performers ready to do it. But in what consists the pleasure to the onlookers? To them the only pleasure and attraction is derived from the consciousness of the danger to which the performer is exposed. Remove them and the

attraction of the performance is gone. These and all similar performances, such as tightrope dancing and trapeze work without nets, only appear to the lowest instincts of a man's nature, and are in a sense educationally degrading. My own opinion is that all matters such as this need most careful supervision. Parachute descents should be forbidden.'

This view was supported by Mr Caleb Hackney in a later edition of the paper: *'Can not public opinion, perhaps supported by some exalted personage, put an end to parachute descents by females? As a last resort there is Parliament.'*

What a dull world it would be if it were full of Reverend Pigotts and Caleb Hackneys! One thing was quite clear in my mind – I wasn't going to give up. First, I had to get better.

During those early days my doctor had brought a specialist from London to examine me, but he had said nothing to me of his findings. Then one morning a young locum came up to my room, and as we chatted I asked, "Doctor, I'm feeling so well in myself, when am I going to be able to walk?"

"Oh, haven't they told you?" he replied innocently. "I'm afraid you're not going to be able to walk again. Your doctor has gone to London today to see if he can get you transferred to a hospital for incurables."

I was flabbergasted! "I'm not going to believe *that*! I *will* walk again!" I said emphatically.

Realizing that he had probably spoken out of turn, the young locum hurriedly changed the conversation and shortly left. Once I was on my own, the possible truth of what he had said began to dawn on me. Never to walk again! A hospital for *incurables*!

I burst into tears – just as the familiar and friendly face of Dr Allen appeared round the door.

"Ah, lassie, what's the matter?" he asked.

"They say I won't walk again – but I can't believe it!" I cried.

"Neither do I believe it," he said reassuringly. "But I've been expecting this. Will you let me try an experiment?"

"Yes, of course – try anything you like."

Without another word he left, to return an hour later with a large black box, out of which he took a series of strange-looking objects and wires. Mr and Mrs Hollins and their daughters joined us, and we watched the preparations with muted astonishment and curiosity. The doctor explained briefly that he was going to attempt simple electrical treatment in an endeavour to stimulate a reaction from the damaged nerves and muscles. I had never heard of such treatment before (nor had many other people at that time), but I was willing to try anything, and I had great faith in this kind family doctor.

With the help of my two 'nurses', I was turned over so that I was lying face down. Eight-inch square metal plates were attached to my back and legs. A box containing a large battery and other gadgets was placed on the table. The farmer, having agreed to take part in the experiment, was instructed to hold two parts of the apparatus, one in each hand, in order to form a circuit. Wearing rubber gloves, the doctor busied himself between attending to the battery and its components and manipulating the plates on my body. For a while there was an air of expectancy, but as the minutes dragged on, the atmosphere became tense. Perspiration was dripping from Mr Hollins' rugged face. His wife and daughters watched anxiously. I, unable to see or feel anything, began to fear that nothing was going to happen – that the experiment was a failure.

I was aware of the doctor looking at his watch, then adjusting his machine again. Suddenly I gave a yell as something seemed to jab me in the back!

The doctor, relieved and jubilant, disconnected the battery. Everyone relaxed.

"I had hoped to get a response in half an hour," he explained, "but it has taken forty minutes. Now we must have a *real* session. Are you ready, Charles?"

He reconnected the battery, Mr Hollins took up his position, and for thirty minutes I lay there with a tingling sensation in my back and legs, which gradually increased throughout the session and which I endeavoured to describe to the doctor as he requested. He seemed well satisfied and returned once or twice each day for further sessions of this primitive electric-shock treatment. By the end of the week I was able to sit up, and the colour of my body returned to normal. I was overjoyed, and the family and Dr Allen shared my delight.

The next step was to get my legs moving. Into one of the main oak beams of the 'house place', Mr Hollins drove large iron staples, and through them he threaded a thick rope. Several times each day I would be helped to my feet so that I could reach up and grasp the rope. Then I would pull myself along it while Mrs Hollins and one of the girls, kneeling behind me, would slide my feet one by one across the floor in a walking rhythm, accompanied by words of encouragement in the local dialect that I had come to understand and love:

"Thou art walking, owd Doll... thou art walking!"

By the end of the week I was indeed able to a walk a few steps on my own.

The morning came when my own doctor called to tell me that he had arranged for me to be taken to London. Imagine his surprise when his 'incurable' patient drew back the bedclothes, sat on the edge of the bed and rose to her feet! He could hardly believe his eyes. When he heard what had happened and that I had been treated by another doctor, he appeared angry, said that he would wash his hands of me and left – muttering that I would have received all the necessary treatment in hospital. It certainly could have been no better than the treatment I had already received from this far-sighted country doctor and my devoted band of 'nurses'.

Soon, with feeling restored to my legs, I was able to discard the stretcher-bed and get around in a two-wheeled wicker chair, lent by Squire Phillips. The wheelchair and I were frequently pushed on to a horse-drawn milk float, and in this manner I was taken on visits to the neighbouring farms. On one occasion a new mare was harnessed to the float and driven by one of the daughters. On our return Mr Hollins asked how the mare had reacted. Jenny's reply was one that I have never forgotten: "She dinna cum much a-goin', but she dinna afe goo a-cummin back!"

As I slowly regained the full use of my legs, I began to make arrangements for my 'come-back'. Quite apart from the fact that I did not want to abandon my parachuting career yet, I *had* to get back into the air to prove to myself that I could do it. One of the contracts that I had made before my accident was for a performance at Ashby-de-la-Zouch, where I had many friends who I knew would support me and welcome me back regardless of what had been said in the newspapers. I contacted Captain Gaudron and told him that I would dearly like to fulfil that particular engagement. He agreed and said that he would arrange for a doctor to be in attendance, just in case!

So it was, just eight weeks after my accident, that I journeyed by train to Ashby, accompanied by 'nurse' Becky. Word of my 'come-back' had spread, and what a reception I was given! So many people had gathered to welcome me that it was impossible for us to get out of the station until one of the committee had the bright idea of fetching the band. With them in the lead and clearing the way with a stirring march, I was played out of the station in royal style, with my happy well-wishers falling in behind to escort us to the Royal Bath Hotel.

Captain Gaudron, who had brought my own balloon and parachute from London, was delighted to see me looking so well and mobile again. I was pleased to see him again too, and to draw some confidence from his calm and reassuring manner, for I was in need of a morale-booster! Although I tried not to show it and certainly did not admit to it, I was truly frightened by the prospect of jumping again. I kept asking myself if I was really strong enough yet. Could my legs and back take the shock of another bad landings? And if things went wrong again, would I have the nerve to cope with them? Perhaps I should have waited longer? Yet I knew that if I *had* waited longer, my resolve might have lessened and I might never have taken to the air gain at all. I had to do it, and as soon as possible. It was like the first jump all over again. The fear was in the waiting and the thinking.

When I arrived for the show at the Royal Bath Grounds, I was quite overwhelmed by the warmth of the reception that I received. I was able to greet many dear friends amongst the crowd. The weather too was kind to me, for it was a beautiful day, with little wind.

I still felt extremely nervous as I checked my parachute and took up my position astride the sling, waiting for the take-off. I tried not to show it, but how my heart was pounding as I once again gave the order, "LET GO!"

As soon as my feet left the ground and I was hoisted above the wildly cheering throng, my fears evaporated. How wonderful it was to be lifted so effortlessly into the sky once more; how beautiful the familiar landscape looked in the sunlight; how soothing to swing there so gently, high above it in that remarkable serenity of the skies. I gave myself plenty of height, carefully identified a good landing-area and tugged on the ripping-cord. There was the old thrill of the fall, and the reassuring tug of an opening canopy, I smiled up at it.

There was a twinge of anxiety as I saw the ground coming up. This was the crucial moment. But once again I need not have worried, for my landing was feather-soft. I rose to my feet, so happy to be a parachutist again.

After a further month of happy convalescence at Field Farm, I returned to London and to Aunty with – miraculously – no lasting disability arising from my injury. Life at the Feather Emporium and in the air returned to normal.

And Louie? I did not see her again. By the time that I had returned to Holborn, she had left, to disappear out of my life. I was given to understand that her fiancé had been furious about the whole escapade, and I imagine that he had been instrumental in removing Louie from the Emporium and from the influence of a certain Dolly Shepherd!

There was one interesting aspect of this story that I did not know of until many years later. Whilst I was lying injured at Field Farm, I had of course missed a number of shows for which I had been previously booked and for which Captain Gaudron had been forced to seek replacements. One of those replacements had been my own mother! She had agreed to jump at a show in the London area on the strict understanding between herself and Gaudron that nobody should be aware of her true identity and that *I* was not to know of it. Billed as 'Madame Papillon', she had made an ascent and a descent free of incident. Only shortly before her death in 1954 did I discover this! When I asked her about it then, her response was typical. "You don't know everything!" she said, and would tell me no more!

9

"Don't Come Up Again..."

"I *shall* fly someday – you just wait and see!" These prophetic words were spoken by Cody with his customary enthusiasm and conviction on one of the many occasions when I chatted with him at the Alexandra Palace during the early days of my parachuting career.

"You'll see it in your lifetime," he said of powered flight. How right he was. Why, I have seen men fly to the moon and back in my lifetime. Mind you, in 1903 the immediate ambition was to lift a flying machine just a few feet into the air, never mind the moon!

In 1904 Cody transferred his aerial experiments to Farnborough, to work on military projects. It was there that he built the Army's first airship – the *Nulli Secundus* – which in September 1907 brought London's traffic to a standstill when Cody and Colonel John Capper of the Army Balloon School flew it up from Farnborough in a following wind to cruise slowly at five hundred feet over Hyde Park, along Whitehall and round St Paul's. Unable to make headway against the westerly wind, they were forced to land at Crystal Palace.

Whilst working on the dirigibles, Cody had also developed his ideas for heavier-than-air flight. Surprisingly, the successful flights by the Wright brothers in America had little immediate effect on aeronautical development in Europe, partly because the brothers had been very secretive about their early experiments, but also because the Europeans thought that they had little to learn from across the Atlantic. Colonel Capper, however, had visited the Wrights in 1904 and was able to pass on some useful advice to Cody in his endeavours to master the air. So it was that on 16 October 1908, in his own biplane powered by two 50hp 'Antoinette' engines, Samuel Franklin Cody became the first man to fly in Britain when his 'Army Aeroplane Number One' flew 1,390 feet at Farnborough. He landed in a bit of a heap, but he had flown!

How thrilled we all were to hear of this achievement. For a long time he had been looked upon by many as something of a crank, and I used to get so annoyed when people laughed at some of his early and unsuccessful attempts to fly. He was a fine man, and those of us who knew him were delighted at his eventual success.

Cody's achievement was to some extent overshadowed by the first appearance in Europe of the Wright 'flyer', for just two months previously Wilbur Wright had amazed the public and the aviation world with the demonstrations of his machine in France.

'In these trials,' said the *Daily Mirror* on 13 August 1908, *'the aeroplane has travelled easily and speedily round a racecourse at the command of its pilot, has executed figures of eight in the air, has sailed, soared, and swept round in loops and circles with the consummate ease and grace of a swallow. Other aeronauts are babies by comparison.'*

These 'other aeronauts' were quick to learn from these unsurpassed demonstrations of flight control, which marked a turning point in European aviation. The great French aviators – Ferber, Farman, Blériot, Voisin – applied new ideas to their own machines, and amongst the enthusiasts who flew as passengers with Wilbur Wright whilst he was in France were the British aeronauts Charles Rolls, Frank Hedges Butler and Major Baden-Powell. In December of that year More Brabazon learnt to fly in France on a 'Voisin' to become the first British pilot – Cody still being an American.

In 1909, inspired by the example of the Wright brothers, powered aviation came of age – not of course as a means of general transport but as a new and exciting vehicle for aerial adventurers and sportsmen. Great advances were made during that year. In July Louis Blèriot crossed the English Channel in his flimsy 24hp monoplane, to great public acclaim – tempered by some concern that Britain's insularity was threatened by this new device! This event was followed in August by the world's first 'aviation meeting', held at Rheims in France and dominated by the American Glenn Curtiss and the French aviators. Similar events were subsequently held in England, at Doncaster and Blackpool. Those prophecies that Cody had made at the Alexandra Palace were indeed coming true. He himself indicated the advances that were being made when he flew forty miles in an improved version of his original flying machine.

The following year, I too became involved in a small way in these early attempts to fly like the birds.

I was acquainted at the time with a clever young engineer called John Turnbull, who had seen several of my descents and was one of a group of people with whom I used to go boating on the Thames from Maidenhead to Folly Bridge, or to Tagg's Island. Sometimes we were entertained by the master of farce Fred Karno on his houseboat. In his spare time, John Turnbull was making a glider. He had rented a disused barn on the top of Box Hill in Surrey, which provided an ideal launching-point for his machine. Like many other pioneers, he based his ideas on observations of bird flight, and I spent many Sundays with him on Box Hill, watching the birds soaring and swooping. The spread and movement of the wings and the manner in which they landed were studied meticulously. The use of the wing tips was thought to be of particular importance, and our observations of bird flight often resulted in minor changes being made to the glider's 'fins'.

The machine was made of bamboo and sailcloth, braced with wire. It had no controls. Following the techniques developed by the original 'hang-glider' pilots of the 1880s and 1890s such as Otto Lilienthal and Percy Pilcher, the glider would be controlled and guided by shifting the weight of the body. Actually flying the glider was very much a matter of trial and error – with many errors! With each failure, however, more knowledge was gained. The machine would be transported back up the hill in John's 'Reo' car, necessary alterations or repairs would be made outside the barn, and another trial flight undertaken. The failures were also expensive because, as the glider fell short, it would land in a farmer's field and damage the crops, and a fee of £5 would have to be paid to retrieve the machine. I understand that today's hang-gliding enthusiasts have the same problem!

When John was satisfied with the glider's progress, he decided to add a one-cylinder Gnome engine, and I was thrilled when he invited me to join him for his flight on 22 July 1910.

We booked in at a hotel in Dorking and asked to be woken at 3.30 am, giving no reason for such an early call as we did not wish to publicize our venture. We met in the hall, as pre-arranged, just before four o'clock and made our way to the Reo which had been parked in a stable. It was a fine, fresh morning and, exhilarated at the prospects that lay ahead of us, we chatted happily as we drove towards the barn. We left the car just above the Devil's Elbow and from there walked to the barn and pulled the glider out on its platform.

The sun was shining by the time preparations had been completed, and when we were ready to begin the experiment, we were astonished to find that despite the early hour we had an audience of about thirty people. How they knew of our trials, which had been quite secret, remained a mystery.

The glider was mounted on a four-wheeled platform which we positioned just a few feet from the precipitous edge of the hill. John took up a position similar, I believe, to that used by modern hang-glider pilots, standing on the platform in the centre of the glider, holding the struts with bent arms, so that his head and shoulders were just above the wings. All was ready for take-off. When he gave the word, I vigorously pushed the platform forward to the very edge and then, by means of a rope, pulled it back quickly to give the glider a 'running start'. Off John went to make a short but successful circuit. Then it was my turn. I was less successful. My 'flight' was a rather unstable swoop down the hillside to fall rather than glide into a field below. The experience was all too short for my liking, with none of the tranquility that I had come to associate with flight beneath the balloon and under an open canopy.

Fortunately the machine suffered little damage, and I was unhurt, but I had to wait for John to drive down the hill to 'bail out' his glider! I had no great desire to repeat the experience. Although I was naturally disappointed that my efforts had failed, my companion was very pleased at the outcome of the trials, and he decided to fit a more powerful two-cylinder Green engine before he tried again.

We returned to the top of Box Hill, lifted the machine from the car and carried it back to the barn, by which time we felt ready for some breakfast. We made our way back to the Reo, and there we stood and stared. Our audience had gone, but before leaving they had filled the open vehicle with bunches of wild flowers! A lovely thought, and typical of the attitude shown to the aviation pioneers of that day and age.

Although he continued his experiments and subsequently achieved several powered 'hops' into the air, John was one of many who had neither the time nor the financial backing to keep pace with other aerial pioneers. As he saw the rapid progress that others were making, he became disheartened at his own efforts and eventually gave them up altogether.

In addition to introducing me to the dubious pleasures of flight from Box Hill, John also took me to watch more advanced flying, first at Brooklands and subsequently at Hendon.

The motor-racing track at Brooklands was one of the earliest 'homes' of British aviation, first used by A V Roe. How well I remember my first visit there, when for the first time I saw those flimsy structures of fabric and wood and wire stuttering uncertainly into the air! Later I went to Hendon where Claude Grahame-White was to develop by degrees one of the most famous of the world's pioneer air centres. What exciting places they were, with an atmosphere of dedication and enthusiasm that reminded me of the aeronaut's workshop in the 'Ally Pally' where I had begun my own aerial career. As an aeronaut myself, I was accepted amongst this flying fraternity and was able to mingle freely with the great aviators of the time – men such as Charles Rolls, A V Roe, Gustav Hamel, Geoffrey de Havilland, Cecil Grace, T O M Sopwith and Claude Grahame-White himself – probably the best known of them all following his tremendous and well publicized performance in the London-Manchester race in April 1910, in which he had narrowly been beaten into second place by the Frenchman Louis Paulhan.

An aviator of vision, Grahame-White was one of the first to anticipate the military value of the aeroplane – in the face of great indifference from the military themselves. Similarly, when we chatted about my parachuting experiences, with great foresight he said, "One of these days *we* shall perhaps have parachutes." This was at a time when most fliers were concerned almost entirely with the problems of getting *off* the ground, not returning to it.

What a happy and exciting atmosphere there was amongst the aviators of that time! They were forever tinkering with their machines, overcoming problems and seeking improvements, mainly through the friendly exchange of ideas and often painful process of trial and error. Some were to find fame and fortune in the skies. Others were to fly to an early death. They were adventurers, all of them.

Although by 1910 the aeroplane had captured the aerial limelight, the balloon and parachute were far from finished. The shows that I gave throughout that summer were as popular as ever, and in fact we were active during one of the major aviation events of the year in Britain. This was the first Midlands Aviation meeting, held in Wolverhampton under the auspices of the Midland Aero Club, formed in 1909.

The importance of these early aviation meetings was not only in providing sporting competition for the intrepid pioneers of powered flight, but also in the stimulus that was given to industry and scientific progress in aeronautics. The flying programme included contests for duration of flight, altitude, cross-country, passenger-carrying (largest number!), figure-flying, shortest take-off and bomb-throwing! All these events carried money prizes ranging from £100 to £1,000 for the winners, whilst a trophy was to be given for the highest flight. Grahame-White, A V Roe, Charles Rolls, Cecil Grace and the Honourable Alan Boyle were all there, amongst many other well-known British aviators. It was an exciting three days that I spent amongst such illustrious company, immersed in the excitement and enthusiasm that were features of those heady days.

The balloon enclosure was set apart from and outside the aviation enclosure and the flying course itself at Dunstall Park, and the timing of events had to be strictly observed to avoid accidents. The balloon was entirely at the whim of the wind, and those early aeroplanes had only limited manoeuvrability, so it was best that the two should be kept well apart and not unleashed into the air at the same time. We still had one major advantage over the powered machines – they could not yet fly as high as the balloon. In fact, Cecil Grace won the trophy for the highest flight by achieving an altitude of only 600 feet! Also, we were less affected by the windy weather that prevailed during the meeting and caused the cancellation of some of the events, whereas our ascents and descents were made in the customary successful manner.

As I was carried by the balloon high above Dunstall Park, I had a bird's eye view of some twenty flying machines – mono-planes, biplanes and triplanes – displayed beneath me, drawn up like a collection of toys conjured up by some genius – or crank! How rapidly the times were changing, I mused, for it was less than two years since Cody had first struggled into the air in his 'Army Aeroplane Number One'.

I was used to going up in the basket with fare-paying passengers, but on one occasion at about this time I had rather unusual company. Two young Army officers were introduced to me – Captain Wilkins and Captain Maitland. They were in uniform and were to be no mere passengers. They were going to make their first parachute drop with me. Captain Maitland was no stranger to the air, for he was an experienced balloonist and had in fact accompanied Captain Gaudron on his record-breaking flight to Russia in the *Mammoth* in 1908. Now, as an Army officer attached to the Balloon Section of the Royal Engineers at Farnborough, he had a great interest in the use of the balloon for military purposes.

The two 'novices' chatted quite happily as we prepared for the ascent, and showed no misgivings as we took our positions in the basket. There was no flying on this occasion. We had the sky to ourselves as we ascended, in a fashion that I thought to be so much more leisurely and peaceful than those noisy aeroplanes! Conversation was scant as we sat on the edge of the basket, legs dangling over the edge. Whatever their feelings, the two military men showed no signs of fear. It was natural that I should jump first, and I was followed in quick succession by the two men. We all landed without a hitch, not far from each other, and were driven back to the grounds where Captain Gaudron awaited us. The two officers seemed well satisfied with their experience, but from the conversation that ensued I soon realized that for them this had been no mere 'fun jump'. Captain Maitland, with considerable foresight, could already envisage the future use of the parachute in military terms. One thing in particular seemed to bother him – the trapeze bar. "I could not allow my men to do *that*," he said. "It is too dangerous, and they must have their hands free."

Listening to them discussing the matter with Captain Gaudron, I realized for the fist time that what I had been doing and enjoying over the years could perhaps have some more practical use in the future. Perhaps the days when the parachute was no more than a vehicle for aerial showmen were coming to an end!

With a formal salute and with thanks to both Captain Gaudron and me, the two Army officers departed.

Little did I realize the far-reaching significance of that brief encounter. Captain Maitland was to become a first-class parachutist himself, and I like to think that he caught the 'bug' from me during that descent at Wolverhampton! More importantly, he was to become one of the leading figures in developing the parachute as a life-saver, initially for use from observation balloons during the First World War and subsequently from aeroplanes. The problem of the trapeze bar? Largely through Maitland's initiative, it was eventually replaced by the parachute harness, which was surely a major step forward in parachute development! After the First World War he became a leading figure in the development of airships, from which he made a number of parachute jumps. How ironic that when the *R-38* broke in two over Hull in 1921 there was no time for him or most of the crew to take to the 'aerial lifebelts' that he had developed, before crashing to their deaths in the Humber.

I continued to give shows throughout the summer of 1911, despite increasing pressures on me to give up my parachuting, and even one quite erroneous report in the papers that I was about to do so. My dear friend Mrs O'Brian was one of those who tried to persuade me to do no more, but I was still enjoying it so, and saw no reason to retire. Yet times were changing...

More and more the aeroplane was taking over the aerial stage. It was as though the balloon, in many ways a symbol of the elegance and leisurely pace of Edwardian life, was being supplanted by an exciting but rather brash and noisy newcomer – just as the Edwardian era itself was being ushered out by a new materialism; by a certain social restlessness; by a great deal more hustle and bustle!

Although the heady pioneering days of flight were far from over, by 1911 it was beginning to take on an altogether more serious aspect. It was becoming a business rather than an adventure. It was also beginning to exact a heavy toll. In 1910 thirty pilots had died in the splintered wreckage of their flying machines, twenty-six of them in Europe. Amongst them were Charles Rolls, whose Wright biplane broke up in mid-air during a show at Bournemouth, and Cecil Grace, who was lost without trace over the North Sea whilst competing for a long-distance prize. There was also much talk of war by 1912, and it needed but little imagination to envisage the air as a battleground of the future. Somehow, some of the fun seemed to be going out of the skies...

On a fine evening during the spring of 1912 I prepared myself happily and confidently for a descent from my solo balloon at the Alexandra Palace. As usual I strolled amongst the spectators as the balloon was being inflated, enjoying my conversations with the people, answering their questions and warmed as always by their friendliness. When the time came, I changed into my parachuting outfit, returned to the enclosure and checked my 'chute as carefully as ever. As I waited for the Captain to complete his final preparation of the balloon, I looked up into the sky. There were no clouds. No noisy aeroplanes, either! I would have all that blue space to myself. I was looking forward to it.

The Captain indicated that all was ready. I took up my position astride the sling and tightened my grip on the trapeze bar. The crowd grew silent. All eyes were on me.

"LET GO!" I cried.

As the balloon rose, I timed my short run forward so that I was lifted into the air with scarcely a swing. I smiled down on the receding sea of faces and waved my Union Jack in response to their cheers as I soared out over the twin towers of the Palace, upwards and ever upwards, with the noise and the faces of the crowd, and the grounds of the 'Ally Pally' itself dwindling, dwindling...

From my gently swaying perch in space, alone in my silence, I looked down on the well-known and much-loved landscape: Wood Green... Hornsey... Southgate... a patchwork of familiar and friendly faces. I was very much at peace with the world.

The silence of the sky was suddenly broken. It was a voice. I did not imagine it. It spoke once, quite clearly, then no more.

"Don't come up again, or you'll be killed," it said.

It was quite plain. Just once, it spoke, then left the words echoing in my mind.

"Don't come up again, or you'll be killed."

I looked around me. The sky was empty. I remained quite still, and very calm, swinging there gently in the silence that had returned. I looked down again at the earth below. It was so beautiful. So remote. So peaceful.

"All right," I said out loud to whoever it was who had spoken, then with no emotion and no regret and for the last time ever I reached out for the ripping-cord.

Back on the ground, amongst the congratulations of the crowd, I gave my little silk Union Jack to a surprised and delighted admirer, and my cap to another, and my parachute badge to someone else.

"I won't be jumping again," I told the Captain. He didn't believe it. "Oh yes, you will!" he laughed. But *he* hadn't heard the voice!

As soon as I was back at Aunty's house, I rolled up my parachuting costume and put it in the ragbag. Calmly I told my aunt that my parachuting days were over.

"Thank God!" she said.

I did.

Epilogue
...But Never a Dull Moment!

I had no regrets when – in response to that timely warning – I finally gave up parachuting. I had enjoyed a fine run, and I was after all only twenty-five years old, and life held many more pleasures and adventures for me.

For the next two years I was fully occupied at the Feather Emporium, but still kept in touch with many of my 'admirers' from my parachuting days. Following the boom in feathers worn at the Coronation of King George V and Queen Mary in 1910, business had gone from strength to strength – despite a few bricks hurled through the windows of the Emporium by supporters of the women's suffrage movement, then at its height and trying to draw attention to itself by such acts.

After the death of King Edward VII, who was uncle to the Kaiser and known as the 'Peace-Maker', an uneasiness seemed to penetrate the gaiety and relaxed way of life that we had known during his reign. What was the Kaiser up to now? By July 1914 war clouds were gathering. They burst on 4 August, when war was declared.

Four days later, with men volunteering in their thousands, my sister Wene and I answered the call to join the Women's Emergency Corps. We were trained in first aid and home nursing, signalling, drill by a Grenadier Guardsman, rough riding with the London and Scottish, and driving. Having obtained her first aid and home nursing certificates, Wene left to take a post as nurse in a munitions factory. We were a highly organized and proficient corps, and we were ready to undertake any jobs we were called upon to do, including the driving of ambulances to ferry the wounded soldiers to various hospitals when they arrived at Charing Cross from France. One of my regular all-night duties was to man a horse-drawn canteen, given by Harrods, at Woolwich Arsenal. I was there on the night a zeppelin hovered over us for a full five minutes before moving on and dropping its bombs four miles away; not a pleasant experience! I was one of the first sergeants, and part of my duties was drilling the new recruits. How well I remember doing this outside the Mansion House – and the caustic remarks by the passers-by!

It had been expected that the war would be over by Christmas, but as it dragged on, the feather business, a luxury trade – suffered badly. Aunty insisted on trying to carry on, and on keeping as many staff as she could. Some, however, left and went to factories, and eventually she agreed, in the summer of 1915, that I should take a full-time job that had been offered me in the War Department – driving munitions. For two years I drove my two-ton, gravity-fed Renault lorry, collecting and delivering raw materials and munitions to factories all over London, and many was the strange load that I carried. An occasion I well remember was when I drove to the Royal Mint to deliver, I think, nose-cap forgings. My truck was reloaded and I was told to go to Tilbury Docks. When the officer in charge signed my 'chit', he asked me if I knew what I had been carrying. I didn't. To my surprise he said, "Gold bullion – two whole tons of it!"

Throughout the two years that I was driving for the War Department, I was still doing part-time voluntary work with the Emergency Corps, which at some time during that period became the Women's Voluntary Reserve.

With the advent of particularly heavy casualties in the field, the War Office decided that the large numbers of already trained women could carry out many of the jobs being done by men – so releasing them for combat duties. Thus in 1917 Mrs (later Dame) Helen Gwynne-Vaughn was asked to form the Women's Auxiliary Army Corps (WAAC), and so was born the first of the Women's Services. Women flocked in their thousands to join up, and the majority of us from the Emergency Corps and the Women's Volunteer Reserve transferred to this new Service. When volunteers were called for to go to France, I applied immediately and was accepted as a driver-mechanic. Although an experienced driver, I had to take the RAC certificate in mechanics and driving, and as part of my test I had to change a wheel in Pall Mall!

I was one of a draft of eight WAAC drivers who eventually arrived in Calais for duty with the Army Service Corps, Motor Transport. When we first reported for duty, we were lined up for inspection by the officers and senior NCOs. There was apprehension on both sides. I could read their thoughts. "What have we got here?" they were wondering. We were each given a testing job. Mine was to put a new sleeve valve into a Daimler engine. The men in the workshop all gathered round me, and my every move was watched by critical eyes. When I had finished the job and finally pulled the starting handle (no self-starters in those days!) and the engine purred, a cheer went up. The first hurdle was over, and by the end of the first week we had all been accepted.

Calais was not a cosy corner! We were a target for heavy bombardments – air raids and shelling, both by day and by night. It was sometimes like hell let loose! We were, however, always warned of special night raids – by the Germans themselves. They were so methodical that if a plane from Richthofen's 'Red Circus' swooped very low along the sands at Calais at noon precisely, we knew we were in for it that night! I often thought back to my parachuting days when I saw the first flying machines being built, and I felt sad to see them now bent on destruction.

Our duties often involved us in hazardous jobs, and in the face of danger there was a wonderful camaraderie and resilience, both within the Army and among the civilian population. Twice we came nearer to the Germans than we should have liked. I was driving an Ordnance Officer to take a new breach-block to one of our big guns, but when we arrived he had only just enough time to destroy it, in the face of the oncoming enemy. On another occasion I took the Inland Transport Officer, Colonel Tagg, to Zeebrugge, where the Germans were in retreat, leaving behind them booby-traps and flaming cordite – and their meals still warm! I had many escapes, including a bridge being blown up just after we had crossed it. Once I had to drive with a large live shell cradled in the boot of the car, prior to it being detonated. On another occasion I was forced to stop to change a wheel, much to the annoyance of the officer I was driving to an important meeting at St Omer. When we arrived at our destination, there was a heap of smouldering rubble. The office had been blown up five minute earlier, a little less than the time it had taken me to change the wheel. Life was full of excitement!

So many were my narrow escapes that I seemed to be leading a charmed life. I sometimes wondered if, just as the 'Voice' had warned me to give up parachuting, I was now being protected from other dangers by some divine hand. The worst that happened to me was a case of frostbite, which almost caused me the loss of four toes. They were saved by the surgeon of the 10th Canadian Field Hospital who replaced the bones with those from the amputated foot of a wounded soldier – surely one of the earliest transplants!

During my two years in France I drove officers of all ranks through all parts of the Northern Sector. When the Americans first came to Calais, I was loaned to them for two weeks, driving General Thompson and his staff. One of the journeys was to a forest to meet General (later Sir) Douglas Haig.

At the time of the Armistice I had to take King Albert of the Belgians back to Bruges. When I reported to him, he was sitting on the wing of a flying machine eating bread and cheese and pickled onions! We set off, the King and two of his officers in my car, escorted by two other vehicles. Our unheralded arrival in Bruges is indelibly printed on my mind. The populace, amid a devastated city, went mad with delight at seeing their King, and although I was merely doing my duty, I was greatly affected by their exuberance. I was overwhelmed by the warmth of the handshakes, the embraces and the bundles of notes that were thrust upon me – quite worthless, but the only gifts they had to show their appreciation.

Rumour had it amongst the drivers one day that I was to drive Captain Sedgwick – the Rent and Lands Officer – who vehemently objected to having a woman driver. Within a fortnight he had changed his mind about women drivers and our friendship grew. He was demobbed first, and within six months we were married in Boscastle, Cornwall, by special licence whilst I was in England on leave. I returned to France and was myself finally demobbed on 11 November 1919.

We set up home on the outskirts of Blackheath, where my husband, a charted surveyor, worked as District Valuer for the south-east area of London. We had a daughter, Molly, and settled down to a very happy life. Aunt Mariam came to live with us for her last eight years until she died in 1932.

In the 1930s I became involved in welfare work – quite voluntary of course, as this was before the Welfare State and Social Services. Looking after my five allocated families comprising thirty-three children in all was an experience that brought many heart-breaking problems but also much satisfaction. I came to the conclusion that practical help, understanding and love were more important than money in overcoming many of the difficulties which those deprived youngsters, all under eleven, had to face.

I began the Second World War helping with the evacuation of children and pregnant mothers to the country, then joined the Auxiliary Fire Service as a volunteer. This meant using our own car, with a 'Fire Service' sticker. One 'job', which was unscheduled, I shall always remember. We had been to see my mother in north London and were near the Mansion House in a traffic jam. My husband, turning to the driver of a lorry remarked, "What a glorious sunset." Came the reply, "Cor blimey, Guv, it's no sunset, all London's on fire!" This was the first day of the London 'blitz'. Suddenly the car was commandeered by four firemen who stood on the running board, one clanging a fire bell. We drove straight into the Surrey

Commercial Docks, which were a raging inferno with all the ships ablaze! Having bumped our way over numerous fire hoses and deposited our human cargo, we were immediately commandeered again and had to take another team of firemen to the Woolwich Arsenal which also was ablaze! When the Government ordered that all private cars were to be taken off the road (and put in a garage with all four wheels off!), the Fire Service wanted me to take on full-time paid service, but this I could not do, and turned my attentions to helping with air-raid shelters.

There was a trench-shelter only two minutes from our house, which we used during some of the intermittent raids in the first few months of the war. When the really heavy bombing began in September 1940, I became Shelter Marshal and had to look after the shelter, which was unfinishd and dirty. We cleaned and scrubbed, and with my husband and daughter, we distempered the grey walls a cheery sunshine yellow. In a short while the shelterers had all become a happy 'family', with a night-life of our own – whist, darts, French classes, knitting for seamen, and a library. We had a first-aid bay and a flourishing canteen and ran a magazine called *The Warren Mag*. We celebrated Christmas there, the cooking of the full turkey dinner being shared amongst several shelterers – and we even had a Christening in this shelter. Such was the spirit during the London blitz. This venture proved very successful, and I was asked by the Town Clerk if I would accept an appointment as Deputy Chief Shelter Warden, and shortly afterwards also Shelter Welfare Officer for the Borough of Lewisham.

When my hard-working boss, Mr Wilson, retired through ill health, I was made Shelter Staff Officer. With a war-time population of 150,000, 113 public shelters and 227 blocks of communal shelters to be looked after, organization and day-to-day maintenance kept me more than busy during the day, with most of the welfare work to be done at night. It was an interesting and busy period of my life, always supported by my husband. My daughter was full-time Centre Secretary and Deputy Centre Organiser of the WVS (Women's Voluntary

Services – now WRVS) in Lewisham for the first two years of the War and then she joined the WAAF (Women's Auxiliary Air Force – now WRAAF).

After the war we moved to Bonchurch in the Isle of Wight, where we lived for seventeen years. After my husband died, I moved to Eastbourne, where I still live with my daughter Molly.

Throughout my life I have of course watched with interest the development of the parachute from the simple device as I knew it to one with a multitude of uses today.

The predictions of Claude Grahame-White and Captain (later Air Commodore) Maitland – and indeed of Montgolfier – came true during the First World War. With the canopy stowed in a container and no longer hanging free, and with the parachutist himself strapped in a safety harness instead of clinging to a trapeze bar, the 'chute saved the lives of many 'observers' forced to abandon their tethered balloons on the Western Front and in other theatres of war. Alas, there was a great reluctance amongst the governments of the warring nations to provide a similar means of escape from disabled aircraft. It was not until the closing stages of the war that Germany provided its aviators with the *Heinecke* parachute. Our boys went right through the war without them. How many of those fine young men that I knew died for want of a parachute?

Even when the war was over, there was still a marked reluctance to provide a 'chute for fliers. A major breakthrough came in the 1920s when the Americans pioneered the use of the manually operated parachute, attached to the aviator and opened by a ripcord after he had fallen clear of the aircraft. Leslie Irvin was the first, when he jumped at McCook Field, Ohio, in 1919. Mind you, there were still a lot of people who thought that to fall freely through the air would cause unconsciousness and death. I could, of course, have told them differently! By the end of the 1920s, however, the manually operated parachute had been widely adopted by air forces throughout the world as a life-saver including the RAF in 1926.

It was also used by my successors on the aerial stage – the show-jumpers who thrilled the crowds at the air circuses and pageants of the 1920s and 1930s, just as I had entertained the people at the 'Ally Pally' and at fêtes and shows throughout the country.

In 1939 the parachute went to war again. Not only did it save the lives of thousands of airmen of all nations, but it also became a means of transporting airborne soldiers into battle, of delivering stores and equipment from the sky and of lowering or stablizing deadly weapons.

Since the Second World War we have seen its role as life-saver progress into the jet-age; have seen it used to recover missiles, satellites and men from outer space; have witnessed the development of brake-chutes and anti-spin devices for aircraft; have seen its role as a means of airborne delivery greatly refined and expanded. Above all, I have watched – with amazement and sometimes with envy – the growth of parachuting as a spectacle, and as a pure *sport* from the 1950s.

In the summer of 1974 at Eastbourne, I watched enthralled as high above me seven tiny figures no more than dots in the sky dropped from an aircraft. Trailing smoke, they hurtled earthwards in free fall, guiding their bodies together and apart again before opening their parachute two thousand feet above the ground, then steering them to pinpoint landings around the target cross right in front of the crowd. These were the 'Red Devils', the famous free-fall parachute display team of the Parachute Regiment. I made myself known to them and was thrilled to find an attractive, dark-haired girl amongst them – Jackie Smith, who was to go on to become Britain's first world parachuting champion when in 1978 she won the women's individual accuracy event in the World Championships by scoring ten dead-centre landings in succession!

The 'Red Devils' were such friendly and unassuming young people, just as interested in this old barnstormer as I was in them and all their modern equipment. With so much in common we had a lot to talk about, and when I said how much I envied them and would love to go up and watch a descent from the air, I was invited to visit them at their Aldershot base. The appointed day proved too windy for a flight, but nevertheless I spent a most enjoyable and interesting day with them, with the promise of a flight when they returned to our vicinity in the near future.

In great contrast to this brush with modern skydiving, we managed to combine the Aldershot visit with a nostalgic return to see the four remaining members of the Hollins' family in Staffordshire where I had been so lovingly cared for after my accident in 1908. Becky, my 'nurse' and Frances, the little 'cowherd', were there, Bill, with is wife Beattie, and Bessie with her husband Bill. They remembered my time with them as vividly as I did myself despite a gap of sixty-eight years, and we chatted and reminisced as old friends. It was a touching reunion. We visited Field Farm at Leigh, now fully modernized and owned by a cousin, and we met his mother, who had been there on the day of the accident! I was interested to see that the original staples put into the beams to help me to walk were still there! We also went to the spot by the road where Louie and I had crashed to the ground, and where an ash tree had been planted shortly afterwards to commemorate the occasion. It had become known locally as the 'Dolly Ash' and was now a full and majestic tree, which made me realize just how long ago it had all happened!

My dream came true at the age of ninety – the promise made by the 'Red Devils' was fulfilled when they again came to give a display over Worthing in Sussex in 1976. We boarded their lovely little Islander aircraft at Ripe, and I was seated as co-pilot, complete with headphones, my daughter being at the back with the parachutists. I was thrilled to watch them leap into space at seven thousand feet. Oh, how envious I felt! As the aircraft circled, I was able to see them land spot on under their brightly coloured canopies. After another display at Eastbourne they presented me with the 'baton' which they had passed from one to another during free fall!

What happy days for this old parachutist, and momentous ones too, as between us we spanned nearly a hundred years of parachuting history. However, not everything has changed during that time. As I chatted with these young adventurers, so much in love with their parachuting life, I realized that, although the equipment they use bears little resemblance to my old 'limp parachute' suspended beneath a balloon with its trapeze bar and sling, and although the skydiving skills now enjoyed are beyond anything that I dreamt of in my Edwardian days, the sensations and the pleasures and the rewards are still the same. The sheer exhilaration, the freedom of the skies, the joy of drifting earthwards under a smiling canopy – these have not changed. Nor have the parachutists. They are still the same. In these fine young men I could see Gaudron and Fleet and Smith and Eames and Hickes. In Jackie Smith I could see a young girl making her determined way up the hill to the Alexandra Palace in the spring of 1903, heading for adventures and pleasures untold.

Alexandra Palace

Postscript
Dolly's Story Lives On...

In July 1983 Dolly was the guest of the RAF Falcons when they 'dropped in' at Eastbourne – and what a happy day that was, to learn how the 'free fall' was achieved. "Oh," she said, "I was born too soon, I should love to make a free fall!" Had the 'tandem' jump been in vogue at that time, I think she *would* have made one!

That was her last outing, as she died on 21st September, but during her long life she had had the pleasure of seeing the development of the parachute from a primitive means of descent from a balloon to a sophisticated apparatus used in the jet-age – and was honoured at the end by members of the most highly trained parachute teams in the country. Members of the RAF Falcons and the Army Parachute Regiment's 'Red Devils' attended her funeral, and magnificent wreaths were sent by the British Parachute Association and the Eastbourne branch of the RAFA (Royal Air Forces Association).

My mother did not see the publication of the first edition of this book – she tried to resist it being written, except, eventually, for 'home consumption' – though we did have great fun during the drafting period! "A lot of fuss over nothing", she would say. "Look at what they do today! Anyway, no-one would be interested!" However, she did read through the final proofs – the week before she died – and wryly remarked "Well, I suppose it's not so bad" – and then with her lovely smile added "If I didn't have the photos and paper cuttings to prove it, I could hardly believe I really *did* have those adventures. Seeing them in print, it all seems like a dream!" I hope she can look down and realise how interested people *are*, and what a great deal of pleasure and encouragement others derive from her experiences.

Since the publication of the book in 1984 her exploits and adventures have appeared in many magazines, sports journals, and in the opening chapters of numerous other books, especially those whose subjects are concerned with aviation, women generally, and biographies – she is even quoted in novels! Co-author Peter Hearn has continued his literary career and includes her in his lectures and books whenever possible, notably in *The Sky People* and *Falcons*. She is in the *Guinness Book of Records* for having performed the historic first mid-air rescue in 1908, as well as being in other historical record books in America.

Her story lives on and goes further afield via the media. Soon after her death the *Dolly Shepherd Story* was shown on television's *Blue Peter* programme and included in their *Blue Peter Book*, volume 22, as one of the outstanding stories of the year. It is perhaps of interest to record that contact has been made with Louie May's family through her nephew Douglas, who saw the *Blue Peter* programme and wrote to the BBC. Louie had married, she had two daughters, Hilda and Marjorie, and died in 1955. Although the family knew of the parachuting accident, they knew nothing of her former fiancé.

Also on television, in May 1992, a reconstruction of the first mid-air rescue was shown as the opening and only historical event (in which Leo's wife, Mandy, played the part of Dolly) in the first of a series of Leo Dickinson's *Dead Men's Tales*, six nail-biting epics when the parachutes did not function properly! Her history was included in BBC Radio 4's well-known and popular *Woman's Hour* in June 1994, and her book is in the library of the RNIB "Talking Book Service", as well as in most local libraries.

Museums have included her in many exhibitions in various parts of the country, including the RAF Museum at Hendon. She has, however, a permanent display in the Museum at Ashby-de-la-Zouch, in the Beck Isle Museum at Pickering, at the Irvin

Parachute Factory Museum in Letchworth, and in the Red Devils' Museum at Aldershot. At the Alexandra Palace in London she is on a mural in the West Corridor, representing the early aeronauts who featured in the history of the Ally Pally. It was four years after my mother's death that I realised for the first time what a privilege it was to be the daughter of Dolly Shepherd. I was invited, as her daughter, to the Bristol International Balloon Fiesta in August 1987, where I was greeted most warmly, with great enthusiasm, and given VIP treatment. From then on I have had many 'doors opened' and have been offered many privileges that I would not otherwise have had. I have made several balloon ascents, and three free-fall parachute descents (in tandem due to age!). Two were from planes at 12,000 ft. My very first one, at the invitation of Garry Gnapp of Action Enterprise at Peterborough, was in 1987, and shown on *Blue Peter*, in conjunction with the original *Dolly Shepherd Story*. The second was in 1989 with the 'Red Devils' at Aldershot, and the third, a 'thank you' for having given the commentary on the first mid-air rescue in *Dead Men's Tales*, was from the basket of a hot-air balloon at 10,000 ft, ascending from Bath with Leo Dickinson, shortly before he made the historic first flight in a balloon over Everest with Chris Dewhirst, an Australian, on 21 October 1991, Andy Elson and Eric Jones being in a second balloon.

In 1985 I was asked by friends who had known my mother if I would give a talk on her early parachuting experiences, at three or four societies, both locally in Eastbourne and on the Isle of Wight, where we lived after the war until 1963. Now, for over ten years I have travelled the length and breadth of our country and to the Channel Islands, giving illustrated talks and lectures, in a slightly dramatic form, on "The Adventures of an Edwardian Lady Parachutist, Dolly Shepherd", to fascinated and incredulous audiences of all ages and to every conceivable society, from small groups to those of over 400!

This year, 1996, the story has been taken to America, to members at a seminar of the Connecticut Lighter-than-Air Society, and I was delighted it received the same enthusiastic reception as in this country. There I had the privilege of meeting one of the outstanding aeronauts of modern times, Captain Joe Kittinger (ex-US Air Force) who holds many records in aviation and parachuting, including free-falling from a balloon at a height of 102,800 ft and breaking the sound barrier on 16 August 1960. His lecture held us spellbound. My presentation followed four hours later, so members had the unusual experience of having the history of parachuting unfold before them, from the first descent made by André Jacques Garnerin in 1797, through the early trials and perils of the barnstormers of the nineteenth century, using their 'limp' parachutes, to the highly sophisticated free fall of the twentieth century.

My hope is that more and more people will be inspired by this fascinating and unique story of pioneering and courage by a seventeen-year-old girl, before the advent of planes and the harness, and at a time when women's activities were very much restricted. She and a handful of other like-minded women were ahead of their time and were the forerunners of the women of today who are now accepted in what used to be called a 'man's world'.

Molly Sedgwick, 1996

Alexandra Palace – mural

Index